GUN TRUTHS

How Gun Laws Fail

COLDAW PUBLISHING
C. D. Michel
284C E Lake Mead Pkwy, Suite 530
Henderson, NV 89015-5511
calgunlawsbook@coldawpublishing.com

Images Provided Courtesy Of
Guy Smith, Gun Facts, https://www.gunfacts.info

Cover Design: Jason O. Crye
Project Manager/Editing/Layout: Darwin Lopena and Grace Wu
ISBN: 978-0-9884602-8-7
Library of Congress Control Number: 2020944135

Printed and bound in the United States of America
at Color House Graphics, Grand Rapids, Michigan

Table of Contents

Acknowledgments

This book would not have been possible if it had not been for the committment and diligence of the team at Gun Facts, https://www.gunfacts.info/. We are particularly indebted to Gun Facts author and editor Guy Smith, who inspires all in his mission to debunk common myths about gun control and remove propaganda from gun control discussions. We at Coldaw Publishing thank you for your service in illuminating the truths in gun control studies and sharing your expertise with the community.

INTRODUCTION

Gun Truths debunks common myths about firearms, self-defense, and gun ownership. It serves as a reference guide for journalists, politicians, law enforcement, and anyone interested in learning about the topics inflaming the debate about gun control. This debate will become more open, honest, and productive if both sides are more informed.

In a world where the "progressive" mainstream media often tells only one side of a story, and where celebrities are given unwarranted expert status and become influencers on complex topics about which they know little or nothing, it is difficult to separate objective fact from subjective and carefully packaged fiction. Truths from half-truths.

Cognitive science tells us that this is because people are more likely to believe things that they've been repeatedly exposed to, especially easily digestible sound bites from a charismatic speaker.[1] And as any marketing professional can tell you, people respond to an emotionally compelling sales pitch over a fact-based sales pitch any day. Love sells.

---

[1] *See* A. Dechêne, et al., *The Truth About the Truth: A Meta-analytic Review of the Truth Effect*, Personality and Social Psychology Review, 14, 238–257 (2010).

Politicians from all parties, and the public relations professionals and social engineers who advise them, have mastered the manipulation of this cognitive phenomenon. Pre-packaged talking points and sound bites routinely avoid hard facts in favor of catchy quotes. "Spinning" to advance an underlying agenda runs rampant. Our less well-informed society suffers for it. But it sells soap. And it wins elections.

By crafting the narrative, the gun-control lobby has created a subculture rooted in misconceptions seemingly supporting and justifying its agenda—to practically rid this country of firearms. So those behind the gun control agenda advocate "common sense" gun "safety" laws while claiming to "respect the Second Amendment." But each of those terms is relative. "Common sense" tells us the earth is flat whenever we look at the horizon. To the gun control lobby, gun "safety" means not having guns at all and the Second Amendment exists but puts no limits on government infringement of the right to own a gun for sport or to protect your family. "Respecting" such a Second Amendment is not really respecting anything at all. Granted, at the existential level, most "truth" is different for each individual because we all see the world somewhat differently. Getting past the ego bias to the objective truth is a challenge. But how does one decide for themselves what is true about the polarizing issues affecting our nation? How does one decide where to stand on a topic, like gun control, when ideas and ideologies are changing and developing every day?

This illusory truth effect is in full display when it comes to gun control. But it takes a lot of work to dislodge illusory truths. The average citizen does not have the time to gather all the data and then organize and process mountains of information. So it is easy to be opinionated, but hard to be well-informed. The misconceptions about firearm use and social utility have been repeated so often that they have become embedded in the consciousness of many—to the delight of those behind-the-scenes influencers who intended exactly that.

It takes some funding, an unbiased and critical eye, and great effort to shift through the data points and analyze what they mean. That's where *Gun Truths* comes in. The authors have accumulated studies and evidence from many high-quality independent sources, including peer-reviewed studies, government databases, and more. The data and conclusions were acquired through the hard work of people who seek the whole truth. *Gun Truths* assesses the relationship between the studies and data points and presents the most salient findings to help readers form an unbiased opinion about gun control. Hopefully, the logical presentation of facts and data in this book, untainted by flashy gimmicks or emotional pleas, will cut through the misconceptions created by the gun-control lobby and its professional message crafters.

Gun Truths is divided into chapters based on gun-control topics. Each chapter lists common myths surrounding firearms and those who possess them. Several facts and sources that show the objective truth based on unbiased, well-researched data follow each myth. This should make it easy to find the information you need to form an educated opinion about the specific policy being advocated. So when you hear a politician, celebrity, influencer, or pundit repeat a sound bite about gun control, you can quickly find that myth in this book and decide for yourself.

When it comes to issues like gun control, we don't want to become like lost sheep—following whoever has the shiniest and most ever-present staff. We must think for ourselves. We must independently inform ourselves of the data available when it comes to guns, crime, and the Second Amendment. Only with *informed* engagement in the debate over gun rights and gun control can we hope to develop an approach to combatting gun violence that is operational, administrable, and meaningful for both sides.

###

THE SECOND AMENDMENT LAW CENTER

www.2ALC.org

Our mission at the Second Amendment Law Center is to protect, enforce, and reinforce the Second Amendment's solemn command that our government never unduly restrict law-abiding individuals from responsibly owning and using firearms for sport, hunting, self-defense, and other lawful purposes. We know, as the Founding Fathers learned from hard experience, that the Second Amendment recognizes a natural right to self-defense, to bear arms, and to protect that right from government infringement. This is something that has not waned over time.

The right to keep and bear arms is fundamentally an individual one and not, as many have wrongly claimed, a "collective" right of state governments to arm a state run militia. Whether it be hunting for sustenance or sport, recreational shooting with family and friends, or defense against aggressors both criminal and tyrannical, our basic human freedoms rely on the individual right to bear arms. If that right falls, or if we allow it to be weakened and watered-down beyond recognition, the fundamental freedoms that flow from it will quickly fade out as well.

Second Amendment rights litigation is not easy. Prevailing in what is often a hostile political environment in legislatures and courts takes experience, knowledge, skills, and resources beyond what most lawyers of advocacy groups possess or have access to. Constitutional rights advocacy and litigation is not a new venture for the team of professionals at the 2ALC. For decades, our "A-team" of lawyers, legal and historical scholars, political advisors, and technical experts have been involved in numerous lawsuits on behalf of non-profit advocacy associations such as the National Rifle Association, the California Rifle & Pistol Association, Gun Owners of California, and many others. Our team has also helped industry trade associations, law enforcement organizations, licensed firearm manufacturers and retailers, trainers, shooting ranges, and individual gun owners.

PART I

VIOLENCE PREVENTION

CHAPTER 1

Guns are effectively used in self-defense millions of times each year.

Myth: Guns rarely prevent crime.

Truth:

- According to the Centers for Disease Control and Prevention, Americans use their firearms defensively between 500,000 and 3 million times each year according to almost all major studies on defensive gun. And researchers have good cause to believe that most people do not report defensive gun uses to law enforcement, so the numbers may be even higher.[1]
- The most extensive study on defensive gun uses found that Americans use guns to defend themselves against criminals approximately 2,500,000 times per year.[2] Thus, on average, 6,849 people defend themselves with guns every day, and one

---

[1] See Centers for Disease Control, *Priorities For Research to Reduce the Threat of Firearm-Related Violence* (2013).

[2] Gary Kleck & Marc Gertz, *Armed Resistance to Crime: The Prevalence and Nature of Self-Defense with a Gun*, 86 J. Crim. L. & Criminology 150, 184 (1995), available at

person every 12.6 seconds. The aggregate of 12 different criminology and media surveys of defensive gun use is about 2,000,000 per year.[3]

- In 83.5% of successful gun defenses, the attacker either threatened or used force first.[4]
- In most instances, merely brandishing or threatening an attacker with a gun is enough to thwart an attack. Less than a quarter of defenders need to fire the gun at all.[5] For those that must fire the gun, a warning shot often suffices. One study shows that in 92% of defensive gun uses, the threat of a gun or a warning shot stops the attack.[6] The attacker must

---

https://scholarlycommons.law.northwestern.edu/cgi/viewcontent.cgi?article=6853&context=jclc.

[3] Gary Kleck & Marc Gertz, *Armed Resistance to Crime: The Prevalence and Nature of Self-Defense with a Gun*, 86 J. Crim. L. & Criminology 150, 184 (1995), available at https://scholarlycommons.law.northwestern.edu/cgi/viewcontent.cgi?article=6853&context=jclc.

[4] *Targeting Guns*, Gary Kleck, Aldine de Gruyter, 1997, from the National Self-Defense Survey).

[5] Gary Kleck & Marc Gertz, *Armed Resistance to Crime: The Prevalence and Nature of Self-Defense with a Gun*, 86 J. Crim. L. & Criminology 150, 185 (1995), available at https://scholarlycommons.law.northwestern.edu/cgi/viewcontent.cgi?article=6853&context=jclc.

[6] *Targeting Guns*, Gary Kleck, Aldine de Gruyter, 1997, from the National Self-Defense Survey).

be killed in fewer than one in every thousand instances.[7]

- Among people polled who had used their firearm defensively, 15.7% stated that they or someone else "almost certainly would have" been killed if not for their defensive gun use. 14.2% said they or others "probably would have" been killed, and 16.2% said someone "might have."[8]
- The following chart from Gun Facts illustrates that the number of annual defensive gun uses (2,500,000) is six times that of criminal gun uses (416,350).[9]

---

[7] *Targeting Guns*, Gary Kleck, Aldine de Gruyter, 1997, from the National Self-Defense Survey).

[8] Gary Kleck & Marc Gertz, *Armed Resistance to Crime: The Prevalence and Nature of Self-Defense with a Gun*, 86 J. Crim. L. & Criminology 150, 176 (1995), available at https://scholarlycommons.law.northwestern.edu/cgi/viewcontent.cgi?article=6853&context=jclc.

[9] Rachel E. Morgan, Ph.D. & Grace Kena (Bureau of Justice statisticians), *Criminal Victimization, 2016*, U.S. Department of Justice, at 5, available at https://www.bjs.gov/content/pub/pdf/cv16.pdf.

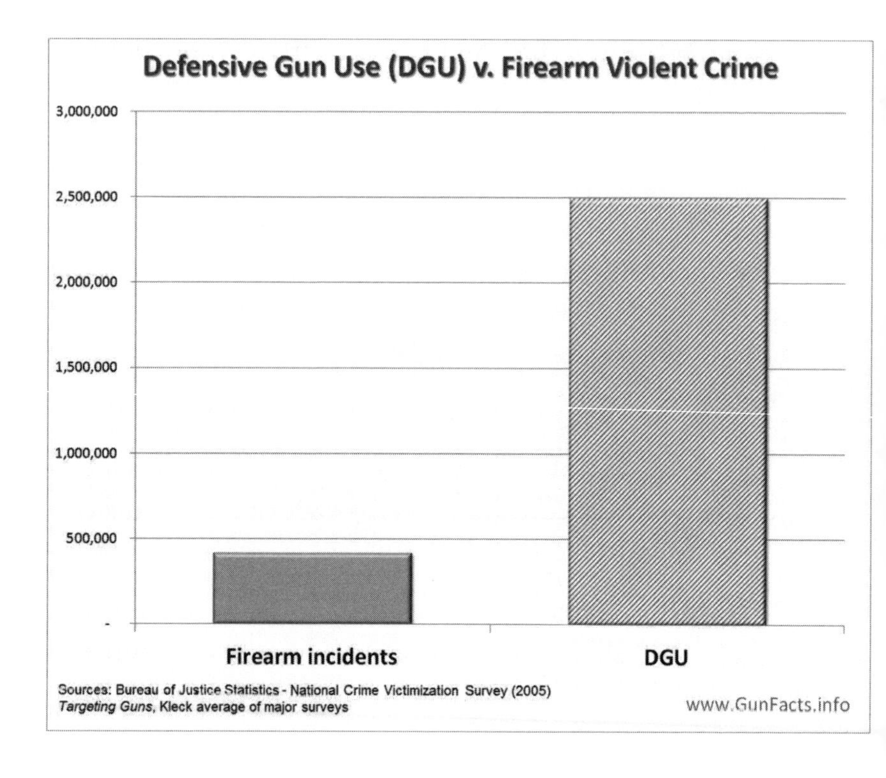

- A 1994 study revealed that within the previous 12-month period, approximately 503,481 incidents occurred in which an armed householder encountered a burglar. In 497,646 (98.8%) of these incidents, the burglar was scared off by the presence of the firearm.[10]

---

[10] Robert Ikeda, et al., *Estimating Intruder-Related Firearms Retrievals in U.S. Households, 1994*, 12 VIOLENCE & VICTIMS 363 (1997), available at available at https://www.hoplofobia.info/wp-content/uploads/2014/05/1997-Estimating-Intruder-Related-Firearm-Retrievals-in-U.S.-Households.pdf.

- Time Magazine followed every firearm homicide in America during the week of May 1 through May 7, 1989. Of the 231 total homicides, 28 (12.1%) were deemed justifiable. Another 16 involved the suspect dying or committing suicide.[11]
- The Centers for Disease Control and Prevention (CDC) reported in 2013 that "self-defense can be an important crime deterrent." Recent CDC reports show that studies directly analyzing the effect of actual defensive uses of guns have found "consistently lower injury rates among gun-using crime victims compared with victims who used other self-protective strategies."[12]
- Gun Facts provides the following chart, showing that victims who used a firearm for self-defense were less likely to suffer an injury than those who used other methods.[13]

---

[11] *Death by Gun: One Year Later*, TIME MAGAZINE, May 14, 1990, available at http://content.time.com/time/magazine/article/0,9171,154482,00.html.

[12] The Heritage Foundation, *Here Are 8 Stubborn Facts on Gun Violence in America* (2018).

[13] *Guns and Crime Prevention*, GUN FACTS, http://www.gunfacts.info/gun-control-myths/guns-and-crime-prevention/.

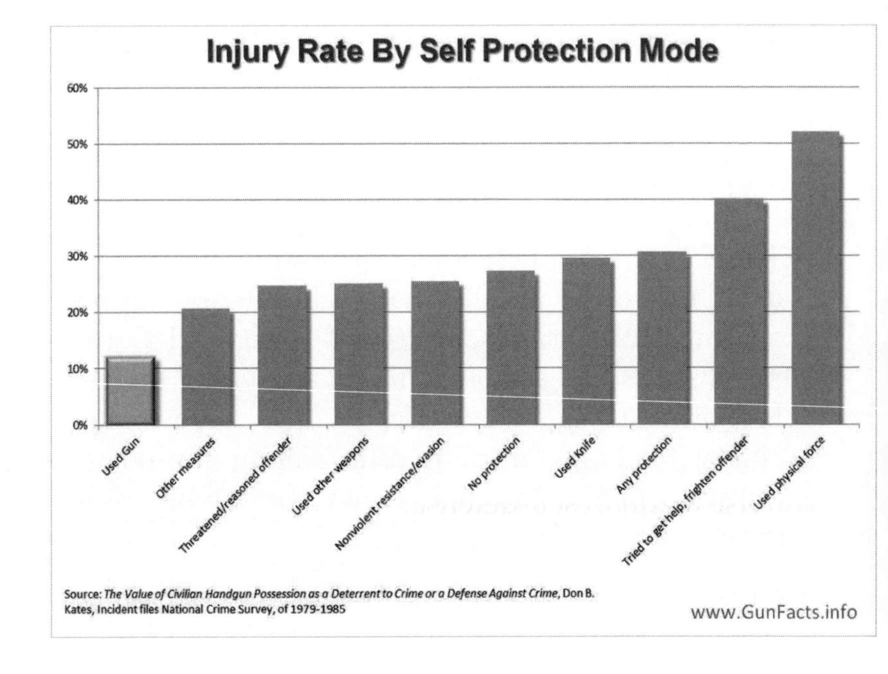
Injury Rate By Self Protection Mode
60%
50%
40%
30%
20%
10%
0%
Used Gun
Other measures
Threatened/reasoned offender
Used other weapons
Nonviolent resistance/evasion
No protection
Used Knife
Any protection
Tried to get help, frighten offender
Used physical force
Source: The Value of Civilian Handgun Possession as a Deterrent to Crime or a Defense Against Crime, Don B. Kates, Incident files National Crime Survey, of 1979-1985
www.GunFacts.info

CHAPTER 2

Using guns in self-defense does not increase your likelihood of injuring or killing yourself.

Myth: You are more likely to be killed or injured if you use a gun in self-defense.

Truth:

- You are very much more likely to survive a violent assault if you defend yourself with a gun.[14]
- For every suicide, accidental death, and homicide with a firearm (29,019), there are roughly 13 times more lives that are saved through defensive gun use (390,000).[15]

---

[14] Don B. Kates, *The Value of Civilian Handgun Possession as a Deterrent to Crime or a Defense Against Crime*, American Journal of Criminal Law (1991).

[15] *See Targeting Guns*, Gary Kleck, Aldine de Gruyter, 1997, from the National Self-Defense Survey); *see also* Centers for Disease Control and Prevention, National Center for Injury Prevention and Control, Unintentional Firearms Deaths (2011).

CHAPTER 3

Guns deter criminals.

Myth: Criminals are not scared of armed victims.

Truth:

- A survey of felons found that "About three-fifths of the sample (56%) agreed" that "a criminal is not going to mess around with a victim he knows is armed with a gun."[16]
- "Four-fifths [of felons] agreed that 'a smart criminal always tries to find out if his victim is armed,' and three-fifths agreed that 'most criminals are more worried about meeting an armed victim than they are about running into the police.'"[17]
- 57% of the surveyed felons agreed that "most criminals are more worried about being shot by their victims than by the police."[18]

---

16 James D. Wright & Peter H. Rossi, *Armed and Considered Dangerous: A Survey of Felons and Their Firearms* 145 (1st ed. 1986).

17 James D. Wright & Peter H. Rossi, *Armed and Considered Dangerous: A Survey of Felons and Their Firearms* 15 (1st ed. 1986).

18 James D. Wright & Peter H. Rossi, *Armed and Considered Dangerous: A Survey of Felons and Their Firearms* 64 (2nd ed. 2008).

- "About two-fifths of the sample [of felons] reported at least one armed-victim encounter at some time in their careers; just over one-third said that they had personally been 'scared off, shot at, wounded, or captured by an armed victim.' About two-fifths reported having decided at least once in their lives not to commit a crime because they had reason to suspect that the intended victim was armed."[19]
- "[T]he highest concern about confronting an armed victim was registered by felons from states with the greatest relative number of privately owned firearms."[20]
- 74% of felons agreed that "One reason burglars avoid houses when people are at home is that they fear being shot during the crime."[21]
- A 1994 study revealed that within the previous 12-month period, approximately 503,481 incidents occurred in which an armed householder encountered a burglar. In 497,646 (98.8%) of these inci-

---

[19] James D. Wright & Peter H. Rossi, *Armed and Considered Dangerous: A Survey of Felons and Their Firearms* 15 (1st ed. 1986).

[20] James D. Wright & Peter H. Rossi, *Armed and Considered Dangerous: A Survey of Felons and Their Firearms* 61 (2nd ed. 2008).

[21] James D. Wright & Peter H. Rossi, *Armed and Considered Dangerous: A Survey of Felons and Their Firearms* 145 (1st ed. 1986).

dents, the burglar was scared off by the presence of the firearm.[22]

- In the United States, victims are home during 27.6% of burglaries.[23] The rate is substantially higher in other developed countries, indicating that burglars are deterred by the possibility of an armed homeowner.
- In 1982, Kennesaw, GA, passed a law requiring heads of households to keep at least one firearm in the house. The residential burglary rate immediately dropped 89% in the first seven months of the ban.[24]
- The following chart from Gun Facts contrasts the legal handgun supply with the property-crime rate from 1973 to 2009.[25]

---

[22] Robert Ikeda, et al., *Estimating Intruder-Related Firearms Retrievals in U.S. Households*, 1994, 12 Violence & Victims 363 (1997).

[23] Shannan M. Catalano, Bureau of Justice Statistics: *Victimization During Household Burglary* 1, 2 (2010), available at https://www.bjs.gov/content/pub/pdf/vdhb.pdf.

[24] 35 Gary Kleck, *Crime Control Through the Private Use of Armed Force*, Social Problems, No. 1., at 15 (Feb. 1998), available at https://americangunfacts.com/pdf/Crime-Control-through-the-Private-Use-of-Armed-Force.pdf.

[25] *Crime and Guns*, Gun Facts, https://www.gunfacts.info/gun-control-myths/crime-and-guns/.

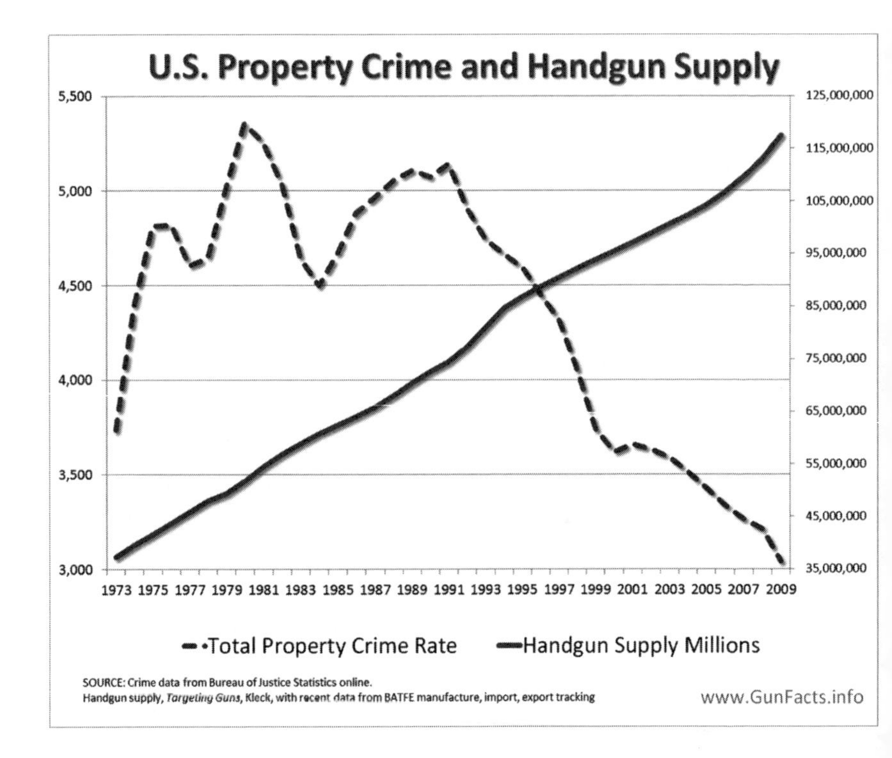
U.S. Property Crime and Handgun Supply
5,500
5,000
4,500
4,000
3,500
3,000
125,000,000
115,000,000
105,000,000
95,000,000
85,000,000
75,000,000
65,000,000
55,000,000
45,000,000
35,000,000
1973 1975 1977 1979 1981 1983 1985 1987 1989 1991 1993 1995 1997 1999 2001 2003 2005 2007 2009
Total Property Crime Rate
Handgun Supply Millions
SOURCE: Crime data from Bureau of Justice Statistics online.
Handgun supply, Targeting Guns, Kleck, with recent data from BATFE manufacture, import, export tracking
www.GunFacts.info

CHAPTER 4

Women frequently defend themselves with guns.

Myth: Women should not use guns for protection.

Truth:

- Women are responsible for 46.3% of the 2,500,000 annual defensive gun uses, despite having lower rates than men of both victimization and gun ownership.[26]
- Guns are used 205,000 times each year for the purpose of defending against rape or sexual assault.[27]
- A study of rape in 26 American cities found that 32% of all rape attacks on a female victim result in

---

[26] Gary Kleck & Marc Gertz, *Armed Resistance to Crime: The Prevalence and Nature of Self-Defense with a Gun*, 86 J. Crim. L. & Criminology 150, 187 (1995), available at available at https://scholarlycommons.law.northwestern.edu/cgi/viewcontent.cgi?article=6853&context=jclc.

[27] Gary Kleck & Marc Gertz, *Armed Resistance to Crime: The Prevalence and Nature of Self-Defense with a Gun*, 86 J. Crim. L. & Criminology 150, 185 (1995), available at available at https://scholarlycommons.law.northwestern.edu/cgi/viewcontent.cgi?article=6853&context=jclc. Table 3 shows that 8.2% of the 2,500,000 annual defensive gun uses occur to prevent rape or sexual assault.

a completed rape, but when a female victim brandishes or uses a gun or knife, the rape is completed only 3% of the time.[28] Alternative defensive measures are less effective, including physical force, trying to get help or attract attention, resisting without force, and threatening, arguing, or reasoning with the attacker.

- Women who do not resist are 2.5 times more likely to suffer a serious injury from an attack compared to women resisting with guns. The benefit to men is also there, but smaller. Men who do not resist are 1.4 times more likely to suffer a serious injury from an attack compared to men resisting with guns.[29]
- A study of 95 completed rapes and 41 attempted rapes committed by men found that "[r]esistance of any kind was associated with incomplete attacks," and that resistance with a weapon in particular made the rape attempt less likely to be completed.[30]

---

[28] M. Joan McDermott, *Rape Victimization in 26 American Cities*, U.S. Department of Justice 31 (1979), available at https://www.ncjrs.gov/pdffiles1/Digitization/55878NCJRS.pdf.

[29] U.S. Department of Justice, National Crime Victimization Survey.

[30] Vernon L. Quinsey & Douglas Upfold, *Rape completion and victim injury as a function of female resistance strategy*, 45 , available at https://citeseerx.ist.psu.edu/viewdoc/download?doi=10.1.1.588.9574&rep=rep1&type=pdf.

- "Analysis of a nationally representative sample of rape incidents reported in the National Crime Surveys for 1979 to 1985" concluded that "The form of resistance that appears most effective in preventing rape completion is resistance with a gun, knife, or other weapon."[31]
- "In 1966 the Orlando city police introduced a gun training program for civilian women in response to an increase in rapes. Although rape was on the increase in Florida and in the United States as a whole, the city of Orlando experienced an eighty-eight percent drop in the incidence of rape during the year following the onset of the gun training program. There was no similar drop in rape rates in surrounding areas and the Orlando decrease was far in excess of any previous one-year change in the city's rape rates, lending support to the hypothesis that the program and its accompanying publicity brought about the decrease in rape."[32]

---

[31] Gary Kleck & Susan Sayles, *Rape and Resistance*, Social Problems, vol. 37, No. 2, pg. 149 (May 1990), available at https://academic.oup.com/socpro/article/37/2/149/1623606.

[32] Gary Kleck, *Policy Lessons From Recent Gun Control Research*, 49 Law and Contemporary Problems 35, 47 (Winter 1986), available at https://scholarship.law.duke.edu/lcp/vol49/iss1/3.

- A Gallup poll found that 58% of women believe that having a gun in the house makes it safer.[33]
- 28.5% of women in the United States have at least one gun in the house, and 41.7% of women say that they have convenient access to guns.[34]
- Dr. Arthur Kellerman, a prolific opponent of defensive gun ownership whose work is often cited by gun control advocates, said: "If you've got to resist, your chances of being hurt are less the more lethal your weapon. If that were my wife, would I want her to have a .38 Special in her hand? Yeah."[35]
- "Firearm availability appears to be particularly useful in avoiding rape. The United Kingdom virtually banned handgun ownership. During the same period handgun ownership in the United States steadily rose. Yet the rate of rape decreased in the United States and skyrocketed in the other countries, as shown in the table[s]" below.[36]

---

[33] Justin McCarthy, *More Than Six in 10 Americans Say Guns Make Homes Safer*, GALLUP, November 7, 2014, available at https://news.gallup.com/poll/179213/six-americans-say-guns-homes-safer.aspx.

[34] T. Smith, National Opinion Research Center, *2001 National Gun Policy Survey of the National Opinion Research Center: Research Findings*, University of Chicago (2001).

[35] A. Japenga, *Gun Crazy*, S.F. EXAMINER, THIS WORLD (Supp.), Apr. 3, 1994, at 7, 13.

[36] *Guns and Crime Prevention*, GUN FACTS, http://www.gunfacts.info/gun-control-myths/guns-and-crime-prevention/ (last visited May 12, 2019).

Reported Rape Rates 1995--2003 (per 100,000 population)			
	1995	2003	% Change
Australia	72.5	91.7	+26.5
United Kingdom	43.3	69.2	+59.8
United States	37.1	32.1	-13.5

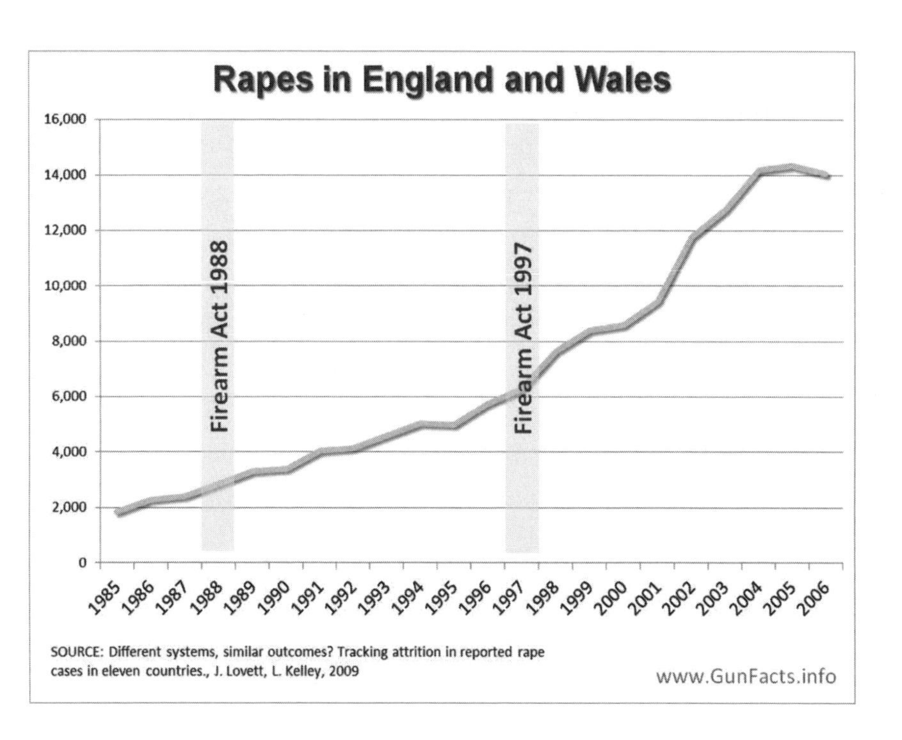

CHAPTER 5

Police cannot always be depended on for protection.

Myth: Only law enforcement should be armed.

Truth:

- The police do not have a constitutional duty to protect people or prevent crime. The Supreme Court has ruled that a victim "did not, for purposes of the Due Process Clause, have a property interest in police enforcement of the restraining order against her husband."[37]
- The American Bar Association's Standards for Criminal Justice provides that:

> In each and every state there are long-standing statutes that, by their terms, seem to preclude nonenforcement by the police.... However, for a number of reasons, including their legislative history, insufficient resources, and sheer physical impossibility, it has been recognized that such statutes cannot be interpreted literally.... [T]hey clearly do not mean that a police officer may not lawfully decline

[37] *Town of Castle Rock, Colo. v. Gonzales*, 545 U.S. 748, 768 (2005).

> to ... make an arrest. As to third parties in these states, the full-enforcement statutes simply have no effect, and their significance is further diminished.[38]

- Similarly, the District of Columbia Court of Appeals stated that "courts have without exception concluded that when a municipality or other governmental entity undertakes to furnish police services, it assumes a duty only to the public at large and not to individual members of the community."[39]
- A 2002 report produced by the U.S. Department of Education in collaboration with the United States Secret Service regarding school shootings states that, "Despite prompt law enforcement responses, most attacks were stopped by means other than law enforcement intervention."[40] "Just over one-quarter of the incidents were stopped through law enforcement intervention."[41]

---

[38] 1 ABA Standards for Criminal Justice 1–4.5, commentary, pp. 1–124 to 1–125 (2d ed.1980) (footnotes omitted) (cited with approval by *Town of Castle Rock, Colo. v. Gonzales*, 545 U.S. 748, 760–761 (2005)).

[39] *Warren v. D.C.*, 444 A.2d 1, 4 (D.C. 1981).

[40] Bryan Vossekuil, *The Final Report and Findings of the Safe School Initiative: Implications for the Prevention of School Attacks in the United States*, United States Secret Service and United States Department of Education 27 (2002).

[41] Bryan Vossekuil, *The Final Report and Findings of the Safe School Initiative: Implications for the Prevention of School Attacks in the United States*, United States Secret Service and United States Department of Education 28 (2002).

- A study of firearm incidents in Missouri found that civilians successfully wounded, drove off, or captured criminals 83% of the times they attempted to do so, while police successfully did so only 68% of the times. Moreover, 11% of police shootings involved an innocent person being mistaken as a criminal, compared to only 2% of civilians.[42]
- The sheriff of Cole County, Missouri, Greg White, advocating for campus carry, said: "In actual shootings, citizens do far better than law enforcement on hit potential. They hit their targets and they don't hit other people. I wish I could say the same for cops. We train more, they do better."[43]
- In 2016, 17,250 people were murdered, 130,603 were raped, and 803,007 were assaulted. Certain-

---

[42] Clayton E. Cramer & David B. Kopel, *Shall Issue: The New Wave of Concealed Handgun Permit Laws*, Tennessee Law Review 62:3 (Spring, 1995) 679–757, available at http://www.davekopel.com/2A/LawRev/ShallIssue.htm. As the authors acknowledged, this does not necessarily prove that civilians are more effective at preventing crime than police, as civilians can often decide whether or not to intervene, whereas police feel a duty to do so—this likely lowers the success rate and increases the likelihood of mistakes for police. The study does provide strong proof, however, that civilians are generally very competent crime-stoppers.

[43] Kermit Miller, *Guns to be allowed on campus?*, 13KRCG, July 31, 2009, http://krcgtv.com/news/local/guns-to-be-allowed-on-campus.

ly, law enforcement cannot stop all crime.[44] This makes sense, as there are only 750,340 sworn law enforcement officers (i.e., employees who carry a firearm and badge and have full arrest powers) in the United States, or 2.39 for every 100,000 U.S. residents.[45]

- The Citizens' Self-Defense Act of 2001, introduced in the 107th Congress, explained that "Former Florida Attorney General Jim Smith told Florida legislators that police responded to only 200,000 of 700,000 calls for help to Dade County authorities."[46]
- The Citizens' Self-Defense Act of 1999, introduced in the 106th Congress, explained that "The United States Department of Justice found that, in 1989, there were 168,881 crimes of violence for which police had not responded within 1 hour."[47]
- "Landmark research in several cities has found that . . . [f]ewer than 5 percent of most cities' total

---

[44] *FBI Uniform Crime Reporting 2016,* https://ucr.fbi.gov/crime-in-the-u.s/2016/crime-in-the-u.s.-2016/topic-pages/tables/table-1.

[45] U.S. Department of Justice, *National Sources of Law Enforcement Employment Data*, Oct. 4, 2016, at 2, https://www.bjs.gov/content/pub/pdf/nsleed.pdf.

[46] H.R.31 – 107th Congress (2001–2002), https://www.congress.gov/bill/107th-congress/house-bill/31/text.

[47] H.R.347 – 106th Congress (1999–2000), https://www.congress.gov/bill/106th-congress/house-bill/347/text.

dispatched calls . . . are made quickly enough for officers to intervene or make an arrest."[48]

- A study of emergency calls to Kansas City Police in the mid-1970s "were stunning: *rapid police response led to an arrest in only 3 percent of serious crimes.*"[49] This study "was considered so important and counter-intuitive that it was replicated during the late 1970s in four other cities—Jacksonville, Peoria, Rochester, and San Diego—with funds from the National Institute of Justice. In each case, the findings were identical: *less than 3 percent of reports of serious crime led to arrests as a result of rapid response.*"[50] Researchers concluded that "on an aggregate level, cases in which 911 technology makes

---

[48] Gordon Witkin & Monika Guttman, *'This is 91…Please Hold'*, U.S. News & World Report, June 17, 1996, at 4, available at

https://drive.google.com/file/d/0B3rrdGNfHq39NzA3YzU1MWItNzVjNC00NWQ4LWFmZmEtMDYyMjkxNjIwZjQx/view.

[49] George L. Kelling & Catherine M. Coles, Fixing Broken Windows: Restoring Order And Reducing Crime In Our Communities 94 (1997).

[50] George L. Kelling & Catherine M. Coles, Fixing Broken Windows: Restoring Order And Reducing Crime In Our Communities 93 (1997) (emphasis in original).

a substantial difference in the outcome of criminal events are extraordinarily rare."[51]

- U.S. Department of Justice research on stalking found that 80% of restraining orders were violated.[52] Law enforcement often find restraining orders difficult to enforce and without physical evidence of a violation, some officers will not punish violations.[53]

---

[51] George L. Kelling & Catherine M. Coles, FIXING BROKEN WINDOWS: RESTORING ORDER AND REDUCING CRIME IN OUR COMMUNITIES 94 (1997).

[52] U.S. Department of Justice, *Crime of* Stalking: How Big is the Problem? (1997), abstract available at https://www.ncjrs.gov/app/abstractdb/AbstractDBDetails.aspx?id=163921.

[53] Ellen Sorokin, *Anti-stalking laws usually are unable to protect targets,* WASHINGTON TIMES, Apr. 16, 2000, https://www.washingtontimes.com/news/2000/apr/17/20000417-011107-6192r/.

CHAPTER 6

Armed civilians can thwart active-shooter incidents.

Myth: A "good guy with a gun" never stops a bad gun actively shooting at people.

Truth:

- An FBI Report on the 50 active-shooter incidents in 2016 and 2017 found:
    - "In 10 incidents,[54] citizens confronted the shooter. In eight of those incidents, one or more citizens safely and successfully acted to end the shooting."
        - "In four incidents, citizens possessing valid firearms permits successfully stopped the shooter."
        - In two incidents, citizens exchanged gunfire with the shooter.

---

[54] "The FBI defines an active shooter as one or more individuals actively engaging in killing or attempting to kill people in a populated area." Federal Bureau of Investigation, *Active Shooter Incidents in the United States in 2016 and 2017*, U.S. Department of Justice 2 (2018), available at https://www.fbi.gov/file-repository/active-shooter-incidents-us-2016-2017.pdf/view.

- "In two incidents, the citizens held the shooter at gunpoint until law enforcement arrived."
- "In one incident, a citizen possessing a valid firearms permit exchanged gunfire with the shooter, causing the shooter to flee to another scene and continue shooting."[55]

---

[55] Federal Bureau of Investigation, *Active Shooter Incidents in the United States in 2016 and 2017,* U.S. Department of Justice 6 (2018), available at https://www.fbi.gov/file-repository/active-shooter-incidents-us-2016-2017.pdf/view.

CHAPTER 7

Most law enforcement prefer an armed citizenry.

Myth: Police favor gun control.

Truth:

- The National Association of Chiefs of Police's annual survey in 2017, which "represents a broad cross section of professional command officers involving every state and every size department," produced the following results to the following questions:[56]

1. Should any vetted citizen be able to purchase a firearm for sport or self-defense?
   Yes: 88.58% No: 7.68% N/A: 3.73%
2. Does your department support nationwide recognition of state issued concealed weapon permits?
   Yes: 85.07% No: 11.09% N/A: 3.84%

---

[56] National Association of Chiefs of Police, *30th Annual National Survey Results* (2017), http://www.nacoponline.org/surveyresults.html.

3. Can qualified, law-abiding armed citizens help law enforcement reduce violent criminal activity?
   Yes: 80.57%   No: 14.93%   N/A: 4.50%

- PoliceOne's Gun Policy & Law Enforcement Survey, based on 15,595 responses from verified police professionals across all ranks and department sizes, produced the following results to the following questions:[57]

1. What effect do you think a federal ban on manufacture and sale of some semi-automatic firearms, termed by some as "assault weapons," would have on reducing violent crime?
   Significant: 1.6%
   Moderate: 6.0%
   None: 71.0%
   Negative: 20.5%
   Unsure: 0.9%

[57] *PoliceOne's 2013 Gun Policy & Law Enforcement Survey Results*, POLICEONE.COM, Apr. 8, 2013, https://www.policeone.com/police-products/firearms/articles/6188462-PoliceOnes-2013-Gun-Policy-Law-Enforcement-Survey-Results-Executive-Summary/.

While the police professionals overwhelmingly favored gun rights over gun control, they were less enthusiastic about open carry than other issues. When asked "what is your opinion about the concept and practice" of open carry: 31.1% "support both the concept and practice," while 40.8% believe "[i]t is a valid concept but the practice is misguided." 18.2% think "[i]n both concept and practice open carry is as bad idea."

2. Do you think a federal ban on manufacture and sale of ammunition magazines that hold more than 10 rounds would reduce violent crime?
   Yes: 2.7%
   No: 95.7%
   Unsure: 1.6%

3. Do you think a federal ban on manufacture and sale of ammunition magazines that hold more than 10 rounds would reduce violent crime?
   Yes: 11.5%
   No: 79.7%
   Unsure: 8.8%

4. Would requiring mental health background checks on prospective buyers in all gun sales from federally licensed dealers reduce instances of mass shooting incidents?
   Yes: 31.3%
   No: 44.8%
   Unsure: 23.9%

5. Do you support the concept of a national database tracking all legal gun sales?
   Yes: 23.0%
   No: 70.0%
   Unsure: 7.1%

6. What is your opinion of some law enforcement leaders' public statements that they would not enforce more restrictive gun laws in their jurisdictions?

Very Favorable: 48.8%
Favorable: 22.2%
Unfavorable: 9.6%
Very Unfavorable: 7.2%
Unsure/Neutral: 12.2%

7. If you were Sheriff or Chief, how would you respond to more restrictive gun laws?
   Not enforce and join in the public, vocal opposition effort: 44.9%
   Not enforce and quietly lead agency in opposite direction: 17.2%
   Enforce and publicly support the proposed legislation: 7.9%
   Enforce and quietly lead agency in support of legislation: 10%
   Unsure: 20.0%

8. Do you believe gun buyback or turn-in programs can be or have been effective in reducing the level of gun violence?
   Yes: 11.2%
   No: 81.5%
   Unsure: 7.3%

9. Do you support the concealed carry of firearms by civilians who have not been convicted of a felony and/or not been deemed psychologically/medically incapable?
   Yes, without question and without further restrictions: 91.3%
   No, only law enforcement officers should carry firearms: 4.1%
   Unsure/Neutral: 4.5%

10. On a scale of one to five — one being low and five being high — how important do you think legally-armed citizens are to reducing crime rates overall:
    1: 4.7%
    2: 4.9%
    3: 14.0%
    4: 21.7%
    5: 54.7%

11. What would help most in preventing large scale shootings in public? Choose the selection you feel would have the most impact:
    Improved background screening to determine mental wellness of gun purchasers: 14.0%
    Longer prison terms for gun-related violent crimes: 7.9%
    More aggressive institutionalization for mentally ill persons: 19.6%
    More legislative restrictions on "assault weapons" and ammo magazines: 0.9%
    Tighter limits on weapons sales and transfers: 1.5%
    More armed guards/paid security personnel: 15.8%
    More permissive concealed carry policies for civilians: 28.8%
    Other (please add): 11.4%

12. Considering the particulars of recent tragedies like Newtown and Aurora, what level of impact do you think a legally-armed citizen could have

made? Choose the statement that you feel is most accurate:
Innocent casualties would likely have been avoided altogether: 6.2%
Casualties would likely have been reduced: 80.0%
There would have been no difference in outcome: 4.1%
An active gunfight might have resulted in greater loss of innocent lives: 5.5%
Unsure or prefer not to answer: 4.3%

13. Do you support arming teachers and/or school administrators who volunteer to carry at their school? Choose the statement you most agree with:
Yes, if they are vetted, trained, and qualified annually: 76.6%
Yes, if they pass a one-time police-level proficiency check: 4.7%
No, only sworn school resource officers should be armed: 15.8%
No, our schools should be considered 'gun free zones': 1.5%
Unsure/No: 1.3%

PART II
REGULATING CERTAIN FIREARMS AND FIREARM ACCESSORIES

CHAPTER 8

"Assault weapons" are rarely used in crime.

Myth: Assault weapons are favored by criminals.

Truth:

- The firearms covered by the federal "assault weapons" ban of 1994 constituted only 1.39% of all crime guns.[58]
- Only 1.5% of state prison inmates were armed with *either* a "military-style semiautomatic" or fully-automatic firearm during the commission of their offense. Only 1.7% of federal inmates were armed with either type of firearm.[59]

---

[58] Gary Kleck, TARGETING GUNS: FIREARMS AND THEIR CONTROL 114 (2017), available at https://books.google.com/books?id=NCAxDwAAQBAJ&q=1.4%25#v=snippet&q=1.4%25%20of%20recovered%20crime%20weapons%20are%20models%20covered%20under%20the%201994%20&f=false.

This number is based on the two most extensive samples of guns recovered by police: statewide samples from Connecticut 1998–1993 and Pennsylvania 1989–1994. "Of the 24,252 crime guns in these samples, 337, or 1.39%, were models covered by the federal AW ban." *Id.*

[59] U.S. Department of Justice: Bureau of Justice Statistics, *Firearm Use by Offenders* 2 (2001), https://www.bjs.gov/content/pub/pdf/fuo.pdf.

- Of the 14.8% of federal inmates who possessed a firearm during their offense, only 9.3% possessed a "military-style semiautomatic." Of the 18.4% of state inmates who possessed a firearm during their offense, only 6.8% possessed a "military-style semiautomatic." Between the federal and state inmates combined, a mere 7% of those who were armed possessed a "military-style semiautomatic." By comparison, 8 in 10 carried a handgun.[60]
- A National Institute of Justice study explained that "studies before the ban generally found that between less than 1 and 8 percent of gun crimes involved assault weapons, depending on the specific definition and data source used."[61] An update to the study clarified that, "AWs were used in only a small fraction of gun crimes prior to the ban: about 2% according to most studies and no more

---

It made little sense for the Department of Justice to combine "military-style semiautomatics" and fully-automatic weapons, as they have little in common besides being used very rarely in crime. The "military-style semiautomatics," function like the other firearms included in the survey (except fully-automatics) by firing one round per each pull of the trigger. In contrast, fully-automatic firearms (commonly called "machine guns") fire continuously when the trigger is pressed.

60 U.S. Department of Justice: Bureau of Justice Statistics, *Firearm Use by Offenders* 3 (2001), https://www.bjs.gov/content/pub/pdf/fuo.pdf.

61 Jeffrey A. Roth & Christopher S. Koper, *Impacts of the 1994 Assault Weapons Ban: 1994–96*, NATIONAL INSTITUTE OF JUSTICE, 8,, fn 17 (1999).

than 8%. Most of the AWs used in crime are assault pistols rather than assault rifles."[62] An "assault rifle" is a gun that has the capability to switch between semi-automatic or a fully-automatic mode, and it is often used by the military. In contrast, an "assault weapon" is a made-up ambiguous term invented by the anti-gun lobby in the 1980's for certain semi-automatic firearms.

- New Jersey became the second state to ban "assault weapons" in 1990. Both proponents and opponents of the ban agreed that they were rarely used in crime. Trenton's Deputy Chief of Police, Joseph Constance, was an opponent of the ban. Constance said, "Assault rifles have never been an issue in law enforcement. I have been on this job for 25 years and I haven't seen a drug dealer carry one. They are not used in crimes, they are not used against police officers."[63] The head of New Jersey's bureau of the federal BATF, Dominick Polifrone, was a proponent of the ban. Nevertheless, he admitted, "I've never encountered an assault rifle . . . The guns we have been dealing with are mostly 9-millimeter handguns, .38-caliber pistols and

[62] Christopher S. Koper, *An Updated Assessment of the Federal Assault Weapons Ban: Impacts on Gun Markets and Gun Violence, 1994-2003*, National Institute of Justice 2 (2004), https://www.ncjrs.gov/pdffiles1/nij/grants/204431.pdf.

[63] Deputy Chief of Police Joseph Constance, Trenton, NJ, testimony — Senate Judiciary Committee, Aug 1993, available at Available at https://www.nytimes.com/1993/06/20/nyregion/both-sides-say-trenton-s-ban-on-assault-rifles-has-little-effect-on-crime.html.

25-millimeter handguns, because they're easier to conceal."[64]

- Police were required to begin keeping statistics after the New Jersey ban's implementation. The 400,000 "assault rifles" in the state were used in only "a tiny fraction -- .026 of 1 percent -- of the total" number of crimes.[65] Testifying before the Senate Judiciary Committee, Constance explained, "This means that my officers are more likely to confront an escaped tiger from the local zoo than to confront an assault rifle in the hands of a drug-crazed killer on the streets."[66]
- A survey of Virginia prison inmates in 1992–1993 revealed that none had carried or fired an "assault rifle" during their most recent crime, even though 20% previously owned one.[67]

---

[64] Iver Peterson, *Both Sides Say Trenton's Ban on Assault Rifles Has Little Effect on Crime*. New York Times, June 20, 1993, https://www.nytimes.com/1993/06/20/nyregion/both-sides-say-trenton-s-ban-on-assault-rifles-has-little-effect-on-crime.html.

[65] Iver Peterson, *Both Sides Say Trenton's Ban on Assault Rifles Has Little Effect on Crime*. New York Times, June 20, 1993, https://www.nytimes.com/1993/06/20/nyregion/both-sides-say-trenton-s-ban-on-assault-rifles-has-little-effect-on-crime.html.

[66] James Bovard, Lost Rights: The Destruction of American Liberty 219 (2016).

[67] Kleck, Targeting Guns, at 117; Virginia Department of Criminal Justice Services: Criminal Justice Center, *Guns And Violent Crime* (1994).

- The Assistant Director of California's Division of Law Enforcement, Steve Helsely, wrote a letter in 1988 (just before California enacted the first state ban on "assault weapons") informing a state legislator that a recent study showing that "assault weapons" were rarely used in crimes "confirmed out intuition that assault-type firearms were the least of our worries."[68] Helsely later said publicly that "These kinds of guns don't play a large role in violent crime and they never have."[69]
- "Of the fatal shootings investigated by the Los Angeles Police Department's South Bureau homicide unit in 1990 and 1991, less than 2% involved assault weapons, records show."[70]
- "Similarly, of 341 gang-related, fatal shootings handled by the Los Angeles County Sheriff's Department in 1990 and 1991, 28 were committed with assault weapons."[71]
- "'The fact,' said Sgt. Wes McBride, a sheriff's gang expert, 'is that for all the stink and hoopla and

---

68 Clayton E. Cramer, FIRING BACK 27 (1994).

69 David Freed, *Assault Rifles Are Not Heavily Used in Crimes*, LOS ANGELES TIMES, May 20, 1992, http://articles.latimes.com/1992-05-20/news/mn-272_1_assault-weapon.

70 David Freed, *Assault Rifles Are Not Heavily Used in Crimes*, LOS ANGELES TIMES, May 20, 1992, http://articles.latimes.com/1992-05-20/news/mn-272_1_assault-weapon.

71 David Freed, *Assault Rifles Are Not Heavily Used in Crimes*, LOS ANGELES TIMES, May 20, 1992, http://articles.latimes.com/1992-05-20/news/mn-272_1_assault-weapon.

wheel-spinning that's gone on, (assault weapons) are not a problem in the gang world.'"[72]

- "Nor are assault weapons prevalent among drug dealers, Helsely said. Of 1,979 guns seized in 1990 by state narcotics agents, he said, only 58 are on California's list of banned assault weapons."[73]
- "In Orange County, six of 199 guns examined by the sheriff's crime lab were assault weapons, according to documents obtained by The Times. In Huntington Beach, seven of 264 firearms examined in 1990 by that city's crime lab were found to be on the list of banned weapons. In San Diego, police analysts logged two assault weapons among the 127 guns they examined in 1990. . . . ."[74]
- "[E]ven a spokesman for Handgun Control, Inc., which advocated tighter restrictions on AWs, conceded that assault weapons 'play a small role in overall violent crime.'"[75]

---

[72] David Freed, *Assault Rifles Are Not Heavily Used in Crimes*, Los Angeles Times, May 20, 1992, http://articles.latimes.com/1992-05-20/news/mn-272_1_assault-weapon.

[73] David Freed, *Assault Rifles Are Not Heavily Used in Crimes*, Los Angeles Times, May 20, 1992, http://articles.latimes.com/1992-05-20/news/mn-272_1_assault-weapon.

[74] David Freed, *Assault Rifles Are Not Heavily Used in Crimes*, Los Angeles Times, May 20, 1992, http://articles.latimes.com/1992-05-20/news/mn-272_1_assault-weapon.

[75] Gary Kleck, Point Blank: Guns and Violence in America 73 (1991) (quoting New York Times 4-7-89, p. A15).

CHAPTER 9

The federal "assault weapons" ban was ineffective.

Myth: The federal ban on "assault weapons" from 1994 to 2004 reduced crime and mass-shootings.

Truth:

- An analysis of crime from 1980–2009 found that "Murder rates were 19.3% higher when the Federal [assault weapons] ban was in effect."[76] "It was also found that assault weapons bans did not significantly affect murder rates at the state level."[77]

---

[76] Mark Guis, *An examination of the effects of concealed weapons laws and assault weapons bans on state-level murder rates*, Applied Economics Letters, Vol 21, No. 4, at 267 (March 2014), available at https://www.researchgate.net/publication/263079249_An_examination_of_the_effects_of_concealed_weapons_laws_and_assault_weapons_bans_on_state-level_murder_rates#pf4.

[77] Mark Guis, *An examination of the effects of concealed weapons laws and assault weapons bans on state-level murder rates*, Applied Economics Letters, Vol 21, No. 4, at 265 (March 2014), available at https://www.researchgate.net/publication/263079249_An_examination_of_the_effects_of_concealed_weapons_laws_and_assault_weapons_bans_on_state-level_murder_rates#pf4.

- A National Institute of Justice study found that "The [assault weapons] ban has failed to reduce the average number of victims per gun murder incident or multiple gunshot wound victims."[78]
- The 1999 study further concluded that "The public safety benefits of the 1994 ban have not yet been demonstrated."[79] One factor that "posed challenges in discerning the effects of the ban" was "the fact that the banned weapons and magazines were rarely used to commit murders in this country" even before the ban.[80]
- An updated study in 2004 found that "the ban has not yet reduced the use of LCMs in crime." And concluded that "we cannot clearly credit the ban with any of the nation's recent drop in gun violence."[81]

---

78 Jeffrey A. Roth & Christopher S. Koper, *Impacts of the 1994 Assault Weapons Ban: 1994–96*, National Institute of Justice, 2 (1999), https://www.ncjrs.gov/pdffiles1/173405.pdf.

79 Jeffrey A. Roth & Christopher S. Koper, *Impacts of the 1994 Assault Weapons Ban: 1994–96*, National Institute of Justice, 10 (1999), https://www.ncjrs.gov/pdffiles1/173405.pdf.

80 Jeffrey A. Roth & Christopher S. Koper, *Impacts of the 1994 Assault Weapons Ban: 1994–96*, National Institute of Justice, 1 (1999), https://www.ncjrs.gov/pdffiles1/173405.pdf.

81 Christopher S. Koper, *An Updated Assessment of the Federal Assault Weapons Ban: Impacts on Gun Markets and Gun Violence, 1994-2003*, National Institute of Justice 2 (2004), https://www.ncjrs.gov/pdffiles1/nij/grants/204431.pdf.

- According to Gun Facts, "In 1994, before the Federal 'assault weapons ban,' you were eleven (11) times more likely to be beaten to death than to be killed by an "assault weapon.'"[82] Additionally, "In the first 7 years since the ban was lifted, murders declined 43%, violent crime 43%, rapes 27% and robberies 49%."[83]

---

82 *Assault Weapons*, Gun Facts, https://www.gunfacts.info/gun-control-myths/assault-weapons/ ("Based on death rates reported by CDC and FBI Uniform Crime Statistics and estimating from state-level reporting on the percent of crimes involving types of firearms").

83 *Assault Weapons*, Gun Facts, https://www.gunfacts.info/gun-control-myths/assault-weapons/ (based on FBI Uniform Crime Statistics, Uniform Crime Reporting Statistics - UCR Data Online, 1995-2012).

CHAPTER 10

"Assault weapons" are popular because of their versatility.

Myth: "Assault weapons" are only good for quickly killing large numbers of people quickly.

Truth:

- Americans own millions of this type of firearms for a variety of lawful purposes, including:

  1. Small game hunting;
  2. Competitive shooting (including the popular 3-Gun competition);
  3. Recreational shooting;
  4. Customization;
  5. Self-defense.

- Their light weight and durability make them suitable for many types of hunting. Time Magazine noted the popularity of AR-15s for hunting feral goats, feral pigs, elk, wild boar, deer, antelope jackrabbits, and coyotes.[84]

---

[84] Will Drabold, *Here Are 7 Animals Hunters Kill Using an AR-15*, TIME, July 6, 2016, HTTP://TIME.COM/4390506/GUN-CONTROL-AR-15-SEMIAUTOMATIC-RIFLES/.

- Persons of small stature and limited strength prefer these weapons because of their relatively light recoil and weight.
- There are many reasons people prefer to use these firearms:

  1. They are easy to operate;
  2. They are reliable in outdoor conditions (backpacking, hunting, etc.);
  3. They are accurate;
  4. They are favored for recreational and competitive target shooting;
  5. They have value in many different types of self-defense situations.

- There are many sports that require these firearms, including:

  1. Hunting;
  2. 3-Gun;
  3. Camp Perry competitions, especially the Service Rifle events;
  4. DCM/CMP competitions;
  5. Bodyguard simulations.

CHAPTER 11

"Assault weapons" are not the most common guns used in mass shootings.

Myth: "Assault weapons" are the overwhelming favorite weapon of mass shooters.

Truth:

- One study found that of the 84 Active Shooter Events[85] occurred between 2000 and 2010, "The most commonly used weapon was a pistol (60%),

[85] The study explained that:

> An active shooter event involves one or more persons engaged in killing or attempting to kill multiple people in an area (or areas) occupied by multiple unrelated individuals. At least one of the victims must be unrelated to the shooter. The primary motive appears to be mass murder; that is the shooting is not a by-product of an attempt to commit another crime. While many gang-related shootings could fall with-in this category, gang-related shootings were excluded from this study because gang related shootings are not considered to be active shooter events by the police (NYPD, 2011).

followed by rifles (27%), and shotguns (10%). This 27% figure includes *all* rifles; so-called "assault weapons" are merely a subset of these.[86]

[86] J. Pete Blair & M. Hunter Martaindale, *United States Active Shooter Events from 2000 to 2010: Training and Equipment Implications*, ADVANCED LAW ENFORCEMENT RAPID RESPONSE TRAINING 2 (Texas State University, 2013), https://rems.ed.gov/docs/UnitedStatesActiveShooterEventsFrom2000to2010.pdf.

CHAPTER 12

"Assault weapons" are not favored by criminals

Myth: "Assault weapons" are favored by criminals.

Truth:

- Only 6 percent of criminals use anything that can be remotely classified as an "assault weapon. What's more, fewer than 2.5% of criminals claim to use such firearms when actually committing their crimes.[87]
- Criminals are over 5 times more likely to carry single shot handguns than they are to carry "assault weapons."[88]

---

[87] Bureau of Justice Statistics, *Firearm Use by Offenders,* November 2001.

[88] Bureau of Justice Statistics, *Firearm Use by Offenders,* November 2001.

CHAPTER 13

"Assault weapons" do not kill one out of five police officers

Myth: One out of five police officers are killed with "assault weapons"

Truth:

- The original study behind this myth included firearms that are not "assault weapons." By including such firearms, the report inflated the statistics. In reality, only 1% of police officers murdered were killed by an "assault weapon."[89]
- Police officers are twice as likely to be killed by their own handgun than they are to be killed by an "assault weapon."[90]

[89] Federal Bureau of Investigation, Law Enforcement Officers Killed and Assaulted, 1994.

[90] Federal Bureau of Investigation, Law Enforcement Officers Killed and Assaulted, 1994.

CHAPTER 14

"Assault weapons" are not "weapons of war."

Myth: "Assault weapons" are "weapons of war" and "only useful in military service."

Truth:

- The gun-control lobby invented the phrase "assault weapon" so that the American public would confuse them with "assault rifles."[91]
- No military in the world uses what are referred to as "assault weapons." By contrast, "assault rifles" are in widespread military use.
- The U.S. Defense Intelligence Agency defines "assault rifles" as "short, compact, selective-fire weapons that fire a cartridge intermediate in power."[92] "Selective-fire weapons" can fire in burst mode and/or fully automatic, meaning that one trigger pull can fire multiple rounds. The Russian AK-47 and the American M-16 rifles are examples. "As-

---

[91] *Assault Weapons and Accessories in America* 26 (Sept. 1988), available at http://www.vpc.org/studies/awaconc.htm.

[92] 5 Harold E. Johnson, U.S. Army Foreign Science and Technology Center, SMALL ARMS IDENTIFICATION AND OPERATION GUIDE - EURASIAN COMMUNIST COUNTRIES 67 (2nd ed., 1970), available at http://031d26d.namesecurehost.com/gunfax/fstcp67.jpg.

sault rifles" are virtually banned in the United States; citizens are prohibited from transferring or possessing any assault rifle that was not already in circulation by 1986.[93]

- "Assault weapons" fire a single shot per each pull of the trigger. So they function like revolvers, lever-actions, pump-actions, bolt-actions, and other semi-automatics, and not like "assault rifles."
- Moreover, "assault weapons" "are no more powerful than other hunting rifles of the same caliber and in most cases are chambered in calibers less powerful than common big-game hunting cartridges like the 30-06 Springfield and .300 Win. Mag."[94]

---

[93] 18 U.S.C. § 922(o) provides:

> (1) Except as provided in paragraph (2), it shall be unlawful for any person to transfer or possess a machinegun.
> (2) This subsection does not apply with respect to--
> (A) a transfer to or by, or possession by or under the authority of, the United States or any department or agency thereof or a State, or a department, agency, or political subdivision thereof; or
> (B) any lawful transfer or lawful possession of a machinegun that was lawfully possessed before the date this subsection takes effect.

[94] *Modern Sporting Rifle Facts*, NSSF, https://www.nssf.org/msr/.

- "[D]uring the 1974-1995 period, when semiautomatic guns were becoming more popular, the fatality rate of gun crimes was generally *decreasing*. Likewise, for an especially well-documented set of shootings, the fatality rate among police officers shot in the line of duty declined sharply from 1988 to 1993."[95]

- The Department of Justice, relying on three different studies, found that criminals did not typically select a firearm based on its type (i.e., shotgun, semiautomatic, revolver, etc.). "In all of the studies, the investigators asked offenders to specify their criteria for selecting firearms. The offenders' responses were similar in all three studies: availability was the overriding factor in weapon choice, and familiarity was the second-most important factor."[96]

---

[95] Gary Kleck, TARGETING GUNS: FIREARMS AND THEIR CONTROL 120 (1997). Kleck explains that "Among gun crimes known to the police, the share that were fatal (i.e., were homicides) declined from 4.3% in 1974 to 3.3% in 1985 and 2.9% in 1995." *Id. See also* Marianne W. Zawitz, U.S. Department of Justice, *Firearm Injury from Crime* 4 (Apr. 1996), https://www.bjs.gov/content/pub/pdf/FIFC.PDF.

[96] U.S. Department of Justice, *Violent Encounters: A Study of Felonious Assaults on Our Nation's Law Enforcement* 45 (Aug. 2006), https://www.fairfaxcounty.gov/policecommission/sites/policecommission/files/assets/documents/pdf/meeting%20schedule%20pdfs/june%2022/band-readahead.pdf.

CHAPTER 15

"Large-capacity magazines" do not make shootings deadlier.

Myth: "Large-capacity magazines" increase the lethality of shooting incidents.

Truth:

- The number of shots fired by criminals has not changed significantly even with the increased capacity of semiautomatics. "For 1985 and 1990 combined, shots per victim was 2.04 for revolvers and 2.53 for pistols."[97]
- Firearm homicides declined from 6.3 to 4.2 per 100,000 population from 1981 through 1998, when ownership of semi-automatics and large-capacity magazines was quickly increasing.[98]
- A study of mass-shootings from 2000 to 2010 found that "Attackers carried multiple weapons in 41% of the attacks."[99] So magazine capacity in mass

---

97 Gary Kleck, Targeting Guns: Firearms and Their Control 120 (1997).

98 Center for Disease Control WISQARS.

99 J. Pete Blair & M. Hunter Martaindale, *United States Active Shooter Events from 2000 to 2010: Training and Equipment Implications*, Advanced Law

shootings does not matter as much. More importantly, mass shootings are rare. The total number of fatalities from mass shootings is less than 0.2% of homicides.[100]

- When mass public shooting incidents and fatalities are mapped out, a distinct pattern emerges. When the shooter uses less than 10 round and 10-14 round magazines, the average number of people killed was 8.0 and 7.1, respectively. Note that fewer people are killed when the shooter uses a "a large-capacity magazine."[101]
- When mass public shooters use 15+ magazines, the average number of people killed was 11.9. This is not a big jump from the 8.0 body count when the shooter does not use any "large-capacity magazine." And given the relative infrequency of mass public shootings, the death rate is still a tiny fraction of all gun homicides.[102]
- Studies show that in most cases, a mass public shooter stops killing people long before he runs out of ammunition in his first magazine, as loca-

---

Enforcement Rapid Response Training 2 (Texas State University, 2013), https://rems.ed.gov/docs/UnitedStatesActiveShooterEventsFrom2000to2010.pdf.

[100] *Magazine Capacity Muckracking*, Gun Facts, https://www.gunfacts.info/blog/magazine-capacity-muckraking/.

[101] *Magazine Capacity Muckracking*, Gun Facts, https://www.gunfacts.info/blog/magazine-capacity-muckraking/.

[102] *Magazine Capacity Muckracking*, Gun Facts, https://www.gunfacts.info/blog/magazine-capacity-muckraking/.

tion and people density are more important factors than magazine capacity when determining death rates at mass public shootings. Nonetheless, politicians continue to inflate the significance of "large-capacity magazines" when it comes to mass public shootings.[103]

[103] *Magazine Capacity Muckracking*, GUN FACTS, https://www.gunfacts.info/blog/magazine-capacity-muckraking/.

CHAPTER 16

"Large-capacity magazines" do not place innocent bystanders at risk for harm.

Myth: "Large-capacity magazines" encourage spray-and-pray fire, putting innocent bystanders at risk.

Truth:

- "Less than 1% of all gun homicides involve innocent bystanders."[104]
- "The odds of a defensive gun user accidentally killing an innocent person are less than 1 in 26,000."[105]

---

[104] Lawrence W. Sherman, et al., *Stray bullets and 'mushrooms'*, Journal of Quantitative Criminology, vol. 5, No. 4 (1989)).

[105] Clayton E. Cramer & David B. Kopel, *Shall Issue: The New Wave of Concealed Handgun Permit Laws*, Tennessee Law Review 62:3 (Spring, 1995) 679-757, available at http://www.davekopel.com/2A/LawRev/ShallIssue.htm.

CHAPTER 17

Microstamping is problematic because every firearm does not leave a unique "fingerprint" after being used.

Myth: Every firearm leaves a unique "fingerprint" that can pinpoint the firearm used.

Truth:

- Research from a group of National Research Council scientists suggests that the technology for collecting and comparing images may not reliably distinguish very fine differences.[106]
- "Not all firearms generate markings on cartridge casings that can be identified back to the firearm."[107] "In 2004 the National Institute of Justice (NIJ) of the U.S. Department of Justice requested that the National Academies appoint a committee of ex-

[106] Daniel Cork, John Rolph, Eugene Meieran, Carol Petrie, BALLISTIC IMAGING, National Research Council, 2008.

[107] Frederic Tulleners, *Feasibility of a Ballistics Imaging Database for All New Handgun Sales*, California Department of Justice, Bureau of Forensic Services, October 2001.

perts to address the issues raised by the computerized ballistic imaging technology."[108] "Underlying the specific tasks with which the committee was charged is the question of whether firearms-related toolmarks are unique: that is, whether a particular set of toolmarks can be shown to come from one weapon to the exclusion of all others."[109] The committee found that "The validity of the fundamental assumptions of uniqueness and reproducibility of firearms-related toolmarks has not yet been fully demonstrated."[110]

- "Also, "[b]ecause bullets are severely damaged on impact, they can only be examined manually."[111]
- "Firearms that generate markings on cartridge casings can change with use and can also be readily altered by the users. They are not permanently defined like fingerprints or DNA."[112]

---

108 Daniel L. Cork, et al., National Research Council, Ballistic Imaging 1–2 (2008), available at http://nap.edu/12162.

109 Daniel L. Cork, et al., National Research Council, Ballistic Imaging 3 (2008), available at http://nap.edu/12162.

110 Daniel L. Cork, et al., National Research Council, Ballistic Imaging 3 (2008), available at http://nap.edu/12162.

111 Frederic Tulleners, *Feasibility of a Ballistics Imaging Database for All New Handgun Sales*, California Department of Justice, Bureau of Forensic Services, October 2001.

112 Frederic Tulleners, *Feasibility of a Ballistics Imaging Database for All New Handgun Sales*, California Department of Justice, Bureau of Forensic Services, October 2001.

- In 2001, California's Department of Justice identified various challenges hampering the feasibility of a ballistics imaging database:
  - "Current imaging systems requite trained personnel, ideally a firearms examiner, for entry, searching, and verification. The use of technicians typically results in higher numbers of false positives that need to be optically confirmed."
  - "Current systems may not be as efficient for rimfire firearms and are limited to auto loading weapons. Proposed systems will not practically accommodate revolvers, rim fires, certain shotguns and rifles. A large proportion of firearms sold in CA may never make entry into the system."
  - "It is unknown at this time whether or not the algorithm can successfully ID a cartridge case fired after atypical break-in and wear have occurred back to the #1 casing fired at the time of manufacture."
  - "All potential 'hits' flagged for further inspection by computer correlation must be confirmed by 'hands on' microscopic examination by a qualified firearms examiner."
  - "Firearms that generate markings on cartridge casings can change with use and can also be readily altered by the user. They are not permanently defined identifiers like fingerprints or DNA. Hence images captured when the firearm

is produced may not have a fixed relationship to fired cartridge casings subsequently recovered."

- "Cartridge casings from different manufacturers of ammunition may be marked differently by a single firearm such that they may not correlate favorably."
- "As the database increases in size, there is an increased potential for a firearm type to be over-represented in the database. As progressively larger numbers of similarly produced firearms are entered, images with similar signatures should be expected that will make it more difficult to find a link. Therefore, this increase does not necessarily translate to more hits."
- "Fired cartridge casings are much easier to correlate than fired bullets."
- "Not all firearms generate markings on cartridge casings that can be identified back to the firearm."
- "Automated computer matching systems do not provide conclusive results."[113]

[113] Frederic A. Tulleners, *Feasibility of a Ballistics Imaging Database for All New Handgun Sales*, California Department of Justice: Bureau of Forensic Services (Oct. 2005), available at http://www.freerepublic.com/focus/news/771039/posts.

- Once a firearm is corroded, a fired round "may not match evidence already on file in databases."[114] "Corrosion is also problematic because some means of dealing with it—including scrubbing with metal or other brushes—may also damage the weapon for the purposes of generating matchable marks."[115]
- A team of ballistics experts analyzed the Remington 30.06 rifle that police believe was used in the assassination of Dr. Martin Luther King, Jr. "Despite 18 test firings and use of high-powered microscopes, the team could not match the rifle with the bullet that killed King . . . The 18 test bullets each had different types of markings. Every test bullet was different because it was going over plating created by the previous bullet."[116]
- George Krivosta of the Suffolk County Crime Laboratory, in discussing the science of Forensic Firearm and Toolmark Examination, explained how much more difficult it is to identify markings left on expended ammunition components than com-

---

[114] Daniel L. Cork, et al., National Research Council, BALLISTIC IMAGING 77 (2008), available at http://nap.edu/12162.

[115] Daniel L. Cork, et al., National Research Council, BALLISTIC IMAGING 78 (2008), available at http://nap.edu/12162.

[116] Gail Gibson & Dennis O'Brien, *Ballistic 'fingerprint' database isn't foolproof tool, experts say*, THE BALTIMORE SUN, Oct. 15, 2002, http://www.baltimoresun.com/bal-te.md.guns15oct15-story.html.

monly believed: "The common layman seems to believe that two bullets fired from the same weapon are identical, down to the very last striation placed on them by the weapon. The trained firearms examiner knows how far that is from reality. The layman might also take as gospel that if you could find a way to place a number onto the tip of a firing pin, then you could certainly read it in the impression. Not until this research was performed and many test fires examined from a firing pin that had a known recognizable pattern, did it become apparent how much change could take place, and why matching firing pin impressions can be so challenging."[117]

- One test of microstamping technology (called "NanoTag") found that 46% of the time, the serial number stamped on the firing pin was undecipherable after ten rounds.[118]

---

[117] George G. Krivosta, *Nanotag Markings From Another Perspective,* AFTE Journal, vol. 38, No. 1, pg. 46 (Winter 2006), available at https://afte.org/afte-journal/searchable-journal-index?title=Nanotag+Markings+From+Another+Perspective&year=&volume=38&number=1&authors=George+G.+Krivosta&keywords=&abstract=&display=normal.

[118] George G. Krivosta, *Nanotag Markings From Another Perspective,* AFTE Journal, vol. 38, No. 1, pg. 43 (Winter 2006), available at https://afte.org/afte-journal/searchable-journal-index?title=Nanotag+Markings+From+Another+Perspective&year=&volume=38&number=1&authors=George+G.+Krivosta&keywords=&abstract=&display=normal.

- Another test "involved subjecting the NanoTag marking to intentional defacement. The entire process was easily accomplished in approximately one minute's time with no special equipment or knowledge needed. In this case, the sharpening stone used was a fifty-year-old stone that was lying around the house."[119] After the successful defacement of the Nanotag identification, "The pistol was then fired with ten Winchester brand .45 auto caliber cartridges and was found to still be operative."[120]
- The National Shooting Sports Foundation and other gun industry representatives "say it could cost up to $150 per firearm." By contrast, the president of the Brady Campaign said it "would cost manufacturers from 50 cents to a dollar."[121]

---

119 George G. Krivosta, *Nanotag Markings From Another Perspective*, AFTE Journal, vol. 38, No. 1, pg. 43 (Winter 2006), available at https://afte.org/afte-journal/searchable-journal-index?title=Nanotag+Markings+From+Another+Perspective&year=&volume=38&number=1&authors=George+G.+Krivosta&keywords=&abstract=&display=normal.

120 George G. Krivosta, *Nanotag Markings From Another Perspective*, AFTE Journal, vol. 38, No. 1, pg. 44 (Winter 2006), available at https://afte.org/afte-journal/searchable-journal-index?title=Nanotag+Markings+From+Another+Perspective&year=&volume=38&number=1&authors=George+G.+Krivosta&keywords=&abstract=&display=normal.

121 Jason Tsai, *Etched Bullets Interest Law Enforcement*, NORTHJERSEY.COM, Sep. 25, 2006, available at http://freerepublic.com/focus/f-news/1708027/posts.

CHAPTER 18

A database of ballistic profiles would not be very useful for tracing crime guns.

Myth: Ballistic databases are massively helpful in solving crimes.[122]

Truth:

- State ballistic databases have been ineffective at solving crimes:
- Maryland
    - As the Baltimore Sun reported in 2016: "Since 2000, the state required that gun manufacturers fire every handgun to be sold here and send the spent bullet casing to authorities. The idea was to build a database of 'ballistic fingerprints' to help solve future crimes. But the system — plagued by technological problems — *never solved a single case*. Now the hundreds of thou-

---

122 "First Lady Hillary Rodham Clinton, running for the US Senate in New York, praised [then-Governor] Pataki for showing 'real leadership in proposing a state-based ballistics program . . . something that needs to be done on a national level.'" Fredric U. Dicker, *Cuomo whacks Pataki gun law*, Apr. 2, 2012, https://nypost.com/2012/04/02/cuomo-whacks-pataki-gun-law/.

sands of accumulated casings could be sold for scrap." "The system cost an estimated $5 million to set up and operate over the years."[123]

- New York
  - The New York Post reported in 2012 that "Despite the hundreds of thousands of spent shells submitted, *not one criminal was ever captured* using the extensive and costly-to-maintain database, state officials concede."[124] "By 2005, New York was spending about $5 million per year."[125]

- A survey of felons found that: "One-half the men in this sample had stolen at least one gun at some time in their lives; many had stolen more than one; a few had stolen guns in extremely large numbers. At least 40%, and perhaps as much as 70%, of the most recent handguns owned by this sample were

---

[123] Erin Cox, *Maryland scraps gun "fingerprint" database after 15 failed years,* The Baltimore Sun, Nov. 7, 2015, http://www.baltimoresun.com/news/maryland/bs-md-bullet-casings-20151107-story.html (emphasis added).

[124] Fredric U. Dicker, *Cuomo whacks Pataki gun law,* Apr. 2, 2012, https://nypost.com/2012/04/02/cuomo-whacks-pataki-gun-law/.

[125] John R. Lott, Jr., *Maryland's long-overdue goodbye to ballistic fingerprinting,* Washington Post, Nov. 13, 2015, https://www.washingtonpost.com/opinions/marylands-long-overdue-goodbye-to-ballistic-fingerprinting/2015/11/13/a277d02a-87db-11e5-be39-0034bb576eee_story.html?utm_term=.5fc2751e430f.

stolen weapons."[126] Because so many crime guns are stolen, tracing them to their last-known legal owner will do little to solve crimes.

- California's Department of Justice found that automated computer matching systems matched bullets to the wrong firearm up to 62.5% of the time, depending on whether the cartridges were from the same or different manufacturers. Cartridge cases were matched to the wrong firearm up to 77.8% of the time.[127]
- Further complicating matters, California's DOJ explained that "Automated Computer matching systems do not provide conclusive results. Rather, a list of potential candidates is presented that must be manually reviewed."[128]
- Ballistic markings can be easily modified. California's DOJ noted that: "Changing the signature of a breech face or firing pin impression for one of the CHP handguns used in this study was a

---

[126] Frederic A. Tulleners, *Feasibility of a Ballistics Imaging Database for All New Handgun Sales*, California Department of Justice: Bureau of Forensic Services (Oct. 2005), available at http://www.freerepublic.com/focus/news/771039/posts.

[127] Frederic A. Tulleners, *Feasibility of a Ballistics Imaging Database for All New Handgun Sales*, California Department of Justice: Bureau of Forensic Services (Oct. 2005), available at http://www.freerepublic.com/focus/news/771039/posts.

[128] Frederic A. Tulleners, *Feasibility of a Ballistics Imaging Database for All New Handgun Sales*, California Department of Justice: Bureau of Forensic Services (Oct. 2005), available at http://www.freerepublic.com/focus/news/771039/posts.

relatively easy affair. The minor alteration required less than 5 minutes of labor to change the signature of the breech face and firing pin. This change is sufficient to make the cartridge case breech face unrecognizable, by IBIS algorithm, to the first set of cartridge cases test fired from that same pistol."[129]

---

[129] Frederic A. Tulleners, *Feasibility of a Ballistics Imaging Database for All New Handgun Sales,* California Department of Justice: Bureau of Forensic Services (Oct. 2005), available at http://www.freerepublic.com/focus/news/771039/posts.

CHAPTER 19

There is no widespread support for a ballistic database among law enforcement.

Myth: "[F]or years police have called for the creation of such a database."
—Sarah Brady, chairwoman of the Brady Campaign[130]

Truth:

- The Fraternal Order of Police is the largest membership organization exclusively for law enforcement officers in the United States, consisting of over 325,000 members.[131] The FOP issued a statement clarifying its position on ballistic databases after the Brady Campaign claimed law enforcement support it:
  - "The FOP does not support any federal requirement to register privately owned firearms with the federal government."

---

130 Jeff Johnson, *Police Challenge Gun Control Advocates on Ballistic Imaging*, CNSNEWS.COM, July 7, 2008, https://www.cnsnews.com/news/article/police-challenge-gun-control-advocates-ballistic-imaging.

131 *Fraternal Order of Police*, https://www.fop.net/CmsPage.aspx?id=223.

- "Without federally-mandated registration of the more than 200 million firearms in the U.S. today, such a database would be no more effective than the current NIBIN [National Integrated Ballistic Information Network] maintained by ATF."
- "In all cases, it is necessary that investigators recover a bullet or shell casing from the crime scene which is intact enough to allow forensic analysis to be able to identify the ballistic markings . . . The firearm must then be recovered in order for the gun and the bullet or shell casing to be conclusively linked."
- "An intact bullet or shell case needs to be recovered from the crime scene, then linked to a gun and then the gun linked to a shooter . . . Ballistics imaging and comparison technology is very limited in accomplishing the latter."
- "Since ballistic imprints, unlike fingerprints and DNA, can be altered, either deliberately or simply through normal use . . . how will we ensure the validity of the findings?"
- "These are law enforcement dollars best spent elsewhere."[132]

[132] Jeff Johnson, *Police Challenge Gun Control Advocates on Ballistic Imaging*, CNSNEWS.COM, July 7, 2008, https://www.cnsnews.com/news/article/police-challenge-gun-control-advocates-ballistic-imaging.

- The Law Enforcement Alliance of America similarly voiced its opposition. Its legislative director said: "A lot of the people who push ideas like this say that, 'Well, even if it just catches one crook it can't hurt,' . . . But if it costs $3 trillion and only catches one crook it sure does hurt, because that's money that could be spent elsewhere on things that we know do work." He added that "It's perfect for the gun control folks . . . It's an idea that sounds wonderful, that - without any education - looks like a neat idea, and the NRA is opposed to it, so it allows them to demonize gun owners over another false issue."[133]
- The Law Enforcement Alliance's chief operating officer said, "One, the barrel is one of the most easily changed parts of many guns and two, the barrel, and the signature it leaves on a bullet, is constantly changing."[134]

---

133 Jeff Johnson, *Police Challenge Gun Control Advocates on Ballistic Imaging*, CNSNEWS.COM, July 7, 2008, https://www.cnsnews.com/news/article/police-challenge-gun-control-advocates-ballistic-imaging.

134 Guy Smith, GUN FACTS 68–69 (2015), available at https://www.gunfacts.info/pdfs/gun-facts/7.0/gun-facts-7.0-screen.pdf.

- Retired Los Angeles County Sheriff's Department detective Joe Horn said: "We in law enforcement know it will not, does not, cannot work. Then, no one has considered the hundreds of millions of guns in the US that have never been registered or tested or printed."[135]

[135] Guy Smith, Gun Facts 68 (2015), available at https://www.gunfacts.info/pdfs/gun-facts/7.0/gun-facts-7.0-screen.pdf.

CHAPTER 20

A ballistic database would be extremely expensive to create and maintain.

Myth: A ballistic database is easy and inexpensive to create and maintain.

Truth:

- "… [A] huge inventory [of possible matches] will be generated for manual review." "[The] number of candidate cases will be so large as to be impractical and will likely create logistic complications so great that they cannot be effectively addressed."[136]
- No state currently requires ballistic imaging through its laws—likely because it has been a costly failure every time it has been tried. [137]

---

[136] Gail Gibson and Dennis O'Brien, *Ballistics '"Fingerprinting" Not Foolproof,* BALTIMORE SUN, October 15, 2002.

[137] See https://lawcenter.giffords.org/gun-laws/state-law/50-state-summaries/microstamping-ballistics-state-by-state/.

CHAPTER 21

"Cop Killer Bullets" were designed for law enforcement and are Teflon-coated to protect gun barrels—not to increase penetration.

Myth: "Cop-killer" bullets are especially dangerous because they were designed to pierce law enforcement officers' body armor.

Truth:

- An experienced police officer drafted an essay on so-called "Cop Killer Bullets," providing the following information:
  - "In the mid 1960's, Dr. Paul Kopsch (an Ohio coroner), Daniel Turcos (a police sergeant) and Donald Ward (Dr. Kopsch's special investigator) began experimenting with special purpose handgun ammunition. Their objective was to develop a law enforcement round capable of improved penetration against hard targets like windshield glass and automobile doors. Conventional bullets, made primarily from lead, are often ineffective against hard targets espe-

cially when fired at handgun velocities. In the 1970's, Kopsch, Turcos and Ward produced their "KTW" handgun ammunition using steel cored bullets capable of great penetration. Following further experimentation, in 1981 they began producing bullets constructed primarily of brass. The hard brass bullets caused exceptional wear on handgun barrels, a problem combated by coating the bullets with Teflon. The Teflon coating did nothing to improve penetration, it simply reduced damage to the gun barrel."

- "Despite the facts that 'KTW' ammunition had never been available to the general public and that no police officer has ever been killed by a handgun bullet penetrating their body armor, the media incorrectly reported that the Teflon coated bullets were designed to defeat the body armor that law enforcement officers were beginning to use. The myth of 'Cop-killer' bullets was born."

- "Congress [] proposed legislation that would have outlawed any bullet based on its ability to penetrate certain bullet resistant material. The FBI, Bureau of Alcohol Tobacco and Firearms, and other forensic experts cautioned that the proposed ban was too vague to be enforceable. The NRA opposed the proposed law since it would have banned not only the controversial armor piercing handgun rounds, but nearly all conventional rifle ammunition as well. The NRA proposed alternative legislation based upon the actual design and construction of the bullets."

- "Gun control advocates and the news media jumped on the NRA's opposition to the original, vague and ineffective proposal. They ignored the NRA's contribution to the final legislation insisting to this day that the NRA wants "Cop Killer" bullets to be available to the public."[138]

---

[138] Mike Casey, *"Cop-Killer" Bullets*, GunCite, Oct. 31, 2004, http://www.guncite.com/gun_control_gcgvcopk.html#ast.

CHAPTER 22

Gun manufacturers are not selling plastic guns that can slip through metal detectors.

Myth: Gun manufacturers are selling plastic guns that can slip through metal detectors.

Truth:

- This myth started in the 1980's when Glock began marketing a handgun with a polymer frame. What people forget is that most parts of this firearm was still metal and, thus, detectable in common metal and x-ray detectors. As a result, "despite a relatively common impression to the contrary, there is no current non-metal firearm not reasonably detectable by present technology and methods in use at our airports today. . . ." [139]

[139] See testimony of Billie Vincent, FAA Director of Civil Aviation Security, House Subcommittee on Crime, May 15, 1986.

PART III
REGULATING STORAGE

CHAPTER 23

Trigger locks requirements are ineffective.

Myth: Trigger locks will prevent children from accidentally shooting themselves.

Truth:

- The government's Consumer Product Safety Commission ("CPSC") tested 32 different gun locks in 2001. "Officials said they believe the sample was a good representation of the locks on the market." "In all but two cases, the locks failed at least one test." The CPSC "found you could open locks with paper clips, a pair of scissors or tweezers, or you could whack them on the table and they would open."[140]

---

[140] Caroline E. Mayer, *Safety Standards Sought After Gun Locks Fail Test*, Washington Post, Feb. 7, 2001, https://www.washingtonpost.com/archive/politics/2001/02/07/safety-standards-sought-after-gun-locks-fail-test/d816ccfb-f282-4f68-bc43-90fdbc399211/?utm_term=.3c66a873d476.

- Children as young as seven years old have shown that they can pick or break a trigger lock; or that they can operate a gun with a trigger lock in place.[141]
- "85% of all communities in America recorded no juvenile homicides in 1995, and 93.4% of communities recorded one or no juvenile arrests (not convictions) for murder."[142]
- A government study concluded that only 7.5% of accidental firearm deaths—a small portion of firearm deaths to begin with—were preventable by child proof devices.[143]
- In 1996, before the implementation of trigger locks laws in many states and when there were around 80 million people who owned firearms, there were only 44 accidental gun deaths for children under age 10, or about 0.0001%.[144]

---

141 United States General Accounting Office, *Accidental Shootings: Many Deaths and Injuries Caused by Firearms Could be Prevented*, March 1991.

142 *Crime in the United States: Uniform Crime Reports*, Federal Bureau of Investigation, 1996).

143 United States General Accounting Office, *Accidental Shootings: Many Deaths and Injuries Caused by Firearms Could be Prevented* 39 (Mar. 1991), available at https://www.gao.gov/assets/160/150353.pdf.

144 Prof. John Lott, CBS News web site, March 20, 2000.

- In 1994, California had a trigger lock law and saw a 12% increase in fatal firearm accidents. That same year, Texas did not have a trigger lock law and saw a 28% decrease in fatal firearm accidents.[145]

---

145 National Center for Health Statistics, 1995

CHAPTER 24

"Safe storage" laws are ineffective.

Myth: "Safe storage" laws protect people.

Truth:

- Deaths caused by accidental firearm discharges were declining before safe storage laws were enacted. "According to statistics maintained by the National Center for Health Statistics, the number of deaths annually caused by accidental firearm discharges has generally been decreasing, ranging from 1,955 deaths in 1980 to 1,501 deaths in 1988. This is a decline of 23 percent over 8 years."[146]
- A comparison of the fifteen states that adopted safe-storage laws between October 1, 1989 and January 1, 1996 with states that had no such laws found that: "The rate of accidental total gun deaths in the two sets of states ends up being virtually the same at the end of the period as when the law passed. The same holds for the subcategory of handgun deaths. Despite these laws potentially being most likely to stop accidental handgun deaths, there is no obvious decline. In fact, while relative acciden-

---

[146] United States General Accounting Office, *Accidental Shootings: Many Deaths and Injuries Caused by Firearms Could be Prevented* 4 (Mar. 1991), available at https://www.gao.gov/assets/160/150353.pdf.

tal handgun deaths fall at first, the relative accidental handgun death rate in states passing the laws almost doubles 4 years afterward."[147] Moreover, "The relative gun suicide rate ends up at almost the exact same level 4 years after adoption as the year that the law is adopted."[148]

- The study also found that: "Our most conservative estimates show that safe-storage laws resulted in 3,738 more rapes, 21,000 more robberies, and 49,733 more burglaries annually in just the 15 states with these laws. More realistic estimates indicate across-the-board increases in violent and property crimes. During the 5 full years after the passage of the safe-storage laws, the 15 states faced an annual average increase of 309 more murders, 3,860 more rapes, 24,650 more robberies, and over 25,000 more aggravated assaults."[149]

---

[147] John R. Lott Jr. & John E. Whitley, *Safe-Storage Gun Laws: Accidental Deaths, Suicides, and Crime,* The Journal of Law and Economics, pg. 667–68, vol. XLIV (Oct. 2001).

[148] John R. Lott Jr. & John E. Whitley, *Safe-Storage Gun Laws: Accidental Deaths, Suicides, and Crime,* The Journal of Law and Economics, pg. 668, vol. XLIV (Oct. 2001).

[149] John R. Lott Jr. & John E. Whitley, *Safe-Storage Gun Laws: Accidental Deaths, Suicides, and Crime,* The Journal of Law and Economics, pg. 686, vol. XLIV (Oct. 2001).

PART IV
REGULATING ACCESSIBILITY

CHAPTER 25

Familiarity with firearms among adolescents should be encouraged.

Myth: Children should have no exposure to firearms before adulthood.

Truth:

- The United States Department of Justice studied gun ownership and criminal behavior among juveniles. It found that:
    - "Boys who own legal firearms . . . are even slightly less delinquent than nonowners of guns." Zero percent of them commit gun crimes, 14 percent commit street crimes, and 13 percent use drugs. Among juveniles who did not own guns, 1 percent commit gun crimes, 24 percent commit street crimes, and 15 percent use drugs.
    - Less surprisingly, there was "a very strong relationship between owning illegal guns and delinquency and drug use." "Seventy-four percent of the illegal gunowners commit street crimes, 24 percent commit gun crimes, and 41 percent use drugs."

- "Boys who own legal firearms, however, have much lower rates of delinquency and drug use and are even slightly less delinquent than non-owners of guns."
- "The socialization into gun ownership is also vastly different for legal and illegal gunowners. Those who own legal guns have fathers who own guns for sport and hunting. On the other hand, those who own illegal guns have friends who own illegal guns and are far more likely to be gang members. For legal gunowners, socialization appears to take place in the family; for illegal gunowners, it appears to take place 'on the street.'"[150]

[150] U.S. Department of Justice, *Urban Delinquency and Substance Abuse* 18 (Mar. 1994), https://www.ncjrs.gov/pdffiles/urdel.pdf.

CHAPTER 26

Most gun control laws are ineffective at reducing crime.

Myth: Gun control laws are effective, and more are needed.

Truth:

- There are countless gun control laws at the city, county, state, and federal level—estimates range from hundreds to tens of thousands.[151] Yet, gun violence remains.
- For a study released in 2016, researchers "analyzed data on 762 cases in which a gun was recovered by the Pittsburgh Bureau of Police Firearm Tracking Unit."[152] "Of the 762 cases, 553 (73 percent) involved a total of 607 perpetrators. Most (n = 478,

---

[151] Glenn Kessler, *The NRA's fuzzy, decades-old claim of '20,000' gun laws*, WASHINGTON POST, Feb. 5, 2013, https://www.washingtonpost.com/blogs/fact-checker/post/the-nras-fuzzy-decades-old-claim-of-20000-gun-laws/2013/02/04/4a7892c0-6f23-11e2-ac36-3d8d9dcaa2e2_blog.html?utm_term=.7878c67581d3.

[152] Anthony Fabio, et al., *Gaps continue in firearm surveillance: Evidence from a large U.S. City Bureau of Police*, SOCIAL MEDICINE, vol. 10, No. 1, at 14 (July 2016), available at http://www.socialmedicine.info/index.php/socialmedicine/article/view/852/1649.

78.7%) were carrying or linked to a firearm that did not belong to them. Eighty-six (14.2%) were owners that committed an offense while legally carrying their firearm, 10 (1.6%) were owners illegally carrying their firearm but committing no other offense, and 12 (2.0%) were owners that committed an offense while illegally carrying their firearm. . . ."[153] So the perpetrator in 79% of cases was a criminal who illegally possessed the firearm. And only 14% of cases involved a law-abiding citizen (that is, until they committed their crime).

- "During 2000–2002, the Task Force on Community Preventive Services (the Task Force), an independent nonfederal task force, conducted a systematic review of scientific evidence regarding the effectiveness of firearms laws in preventing violence, including violent crimes, suicide, and unintentional injury. The following laws were evaluated: bans on specified firearms or ammunition, restrictions on firearm acquisition, waiting periods for firearm acquisition, firearm registration and licensing of firearm owners, 'shall issue' concealed weapon carry laws, child access prevention laws, zero tolerance laws for firearms in schools, and combinations of firearms laws. The Task Force found insufficient evidence to determine the effectiveness of

---

[153] Anthony Fabio, et al., *Gaps continue in firearm surveillance: Evidence from a large U.S. City Bureau of Police*, SOCIAL MEDICINE, vol. 10, No. 1, at 17 (July 2016), available at http://www.socialmedicine.info/index.php/socialmedicine/article/view/852/1649.

any of the firearms laws or combinations of laws reviewed on violent outcomes."[154]

- Reporting on an FBI study of shootings of police officers, Force Science News (of the Force Science Institute) explained: "Predominately handguns were used in the assaults on officers and all but one were obtained illegally, usually in street transactions or in thefts. In contrast to media myth, none of the firearms in the study was obtained from gun shows. What was available 'was the overriding factor in weapon choice,' the report says. Only 1 offender hand-picked a particular gun 'because he felt it would do the most damage to a human being.' Researcher Davis, in a presentation and discussion for the International Assn. of Chiefs of Police, noted that none of the attackers interviewed was 'hindered by any law--federal, state or local--that has ever been established to prevent gun ownership. They just laughed at gun laws.'"[155]
- "In 1976, Washington, D.C. enacted one of the most restrictive gun control laws in the nation. The city's

[154] Robert A. Hahn, *First Reports Evaluating the Effectiveness of Strategies for Preventing Violence: Firearms Laws*, Centers for Disease Control and Prevention, https://www.cdc.gov/mmwr/preview/mmwrhtml/rr5214a2.htm.

[155] *Force Science News #62*, Force Science News, Dec. 28, 2006, http://www.forcesciencenews.com/home/detail.html?serial=62.

murder rate rose 134 percent through 1996 while the national murder rate dropped 2 percent."[156]

- In 2000, there were 15,517 total murders and non-negligent homicides.[157] 12% of these occurred in four cities with roughly six percent of the population—New York (673), Chicago (628), Detroit (396), and Washington, D.C. (239)—which virtually prohibited handgun ownership at the time.[158]
- A study on the decline of crime in the 1990s found "little or no evidence that changes in gun control laws in the 1990s can account for falling crime."[159] It determined background checks, gun buy-back programs, and handgun bans were all ineffective:

---

[156] Gary Kleck, University of Florida using FBI Uniform Crime Statistics, 1997.

[157] FBI Uniform Crime Reporting, Crime in the United States 2000, Section II – Crime Index Offenses Reported 10, https://ucr.fbi.gov/crime-in-the-u.s/2000/00sec2.pdf.

[158] FBI Uniform Crime Reporting, Crime in the United States 2000, table 8, https://ucr.fbi.gov/crime-in-the-u.s/2000.

[159] Steven D. Levitt, *Understanding Why Crime Fell in the 1990s: Four Factors that Explain the Decline and Six that Do Not*, JOURNAL OF ECONOMIC PERSPECTIVES, vol. 18, No. 1, 173–74 (Winter 2004), available at http://pricetheory.uchicago.edu/levitt/Papers/LevittUnderstandingWhyCrime2004.pdf. Levitt also determined that the increase in laws allowing concealed carry had little impact, contrary to the many studies cited in this book.

- "For example, the Brady Handgun Violence Prevention Act of 1993 instituted stricter requirements for background checks before a gun is sold. However, Ludwig and Cook (2000) report no difference in homicide trends after the passage of the Brady Act in states affected by the law and states that already had policies in place that were at least as stringent as those in the Brady Act. Given the realities of an active black market in guns (Cook, Molliconi and Cole, 1995), the apparent ineffectiveness of gun control laws should not come as a great surprise to economists. Even in the late 1980s, prior to the Brady Act, only about one-fifth of prisoners reported obtaining their guns through licensed gun dealers (Wright and Rossi, 1994)."[160]

- "Gun buy-back programs are another form of public policy instituted in the 1990s that is largely ineffective in reducing crime. First, the guns that are typically surrendered in gun buy-backs are those guns that are least likely to be used in criminal activities. The guns turned in will be, by definition, those for which the owners derive little value from the possession of the guns. In contrast, those who are using guns in crimes are unlikely to participate in such

---

[160] Steven D. Levitt, *Understanding Why Crime Fell in the 1990s: Four Factors that Explain the Decline and Six that Do Not*, JOURNAL OF ECONOMIC PERSPECTIVES, vol. 18, No. 1, 174 (Winter 2004), available at http://pricetheory.uchicago.edu/levitt/Papers/LevittUnderstandingWhyCrime2004.pdf.

programs. Second, because replacement guns are relatively easily obtained, the decline in the number of guns on the street may be smaller than the number of guns that are turned in. Third, the likelihood that any particular gun will be used in a crime in a given year is low. In 1999, approximately 6,500 homicides were committed with handguns. There are approximately 65 million handguns in the United States. Thus, if a different handgun were used in each homicide, the likelihood that a particular handgun would be used to kill an individual in a particular year is one in 10,000. The typical gun buy-back program yields fewer than 1,000 guns. Thus, it is not surprising that research evaluations have consistently failed to document any link between gun buy-back programs and reductions in gun violence (Callahan, Rivera and Koepsell, 1994; Kennedy, Piehl and Braga, 1996; Rosenfeld, 1996; Reuter and Mouzos, 2003)."[161]

- "More stringent gun-control policies such as bans on handgun acquisition passed in Washington, D.C., in 1976 and the ban on handgun ownership in Chicago in 1982 do not seem to have reduced crime, either. While initial research suggested a beneficial impact of the D.C.

---

[161] Steven D. Levitt, *Understanding Why Crime Fell in the 1990s: Four Factors that Explain the Decline and Six that Do Not*, Journal of Economic Perspectives, vol. 18, No. 1, 174 (Winter 2004), available at http://pricetheory.uchicago.edu/levitt/Papers/LevittUnderstandingWhyCrime2004.pdf.

gun ban (Loftin, McDowall, Weirsema and Cottey, 1991), when the city of Baltimore is used as a control group, rather than the affluent Washington suburbs, the apparent benefits of the gun ban disappear (Britt, Kleck and Bordua, 1996). Although no careful analysis of Chicago's gun ban has been carried out, the fact that Chicago has been a laggard in the nationwide homicide decline argues against any large impact of the law."[162]

- The following Gun Facts chart demonstrates the relative ineffectiveness of gun control laws compared to the possible or collateral impact of expanded concealed carry rights.[163]

---

[162] Steven D. Levitt, *Understanding Why Crime Fell in the 1990s: Four Factors that Explain the Decline and Six that Do Not*, Journal of Economic Perspectives, vol. 18, No. 1, 174 (Winter 2004), available at http://pricetheory.uchicago.edu/levitt/Papers/LevittUnderstandingWhyCrime2004.pdf.

[163] *Government, Laws, Social Costs*, Gun Facts, http://www.gunfacts.info/gun-control-myths/government-gun-laws-and-social-costs/.

U.S. Homicide Rate per 100,000 Population
Prohibition
Modern American Gun Control Era
Expansion of Concealed Carry Rights
12.0
10.0
8.0
6.0
4.0
2.0
0.0
SOURCE: National Center for Health Statistics, Vital Statistics, Revised July, 1999. 1994 and beyond, Bureau of Justice Statistics online
www.GunFacts.info

CHAPTER 27

One reason why gun control laws are ineffective is because they are underenforced.

Myth: We need more gun control laws because the laws that already exist are not enough.

Truth:

- Regarding enforcement of firearms laws, Gun Facts explains:
  - "During the Clinton administration, federal prosecutions of gun-related crimes dropped more than 44 percent." "Of the 3,353 prohibited individuals that obtained firearms, the Clinton administration only investigated 110 of them (3.3%)."[164]
  - "Despite 536,000 prohibited buyers caught by the National Instant Criminal Background Check System (NICS), only 6,700 people (1.25%) have been charged for these firearms violations. This includes 71% of the violations coming from

[164] *Government, Laws, Social Costs*, Gun Facts, https://www.gunfacts.info/gun-control-myths/government-gun-laws-and-social-costs/.

convicted or indicted felons. None of these crimes were prosecuted by the Federal government in 1996, 1997, or 1998." [165]

- "Half of referrals concerning violent criminals were closed without investigation or prosecution." And "The average sentence for a federal firearms violation dropped from 57 months to 46 months from 1996 to 1998."[166]
- "During Project Exile in Richmond, Virginia, US and State authorities prosecuted felons caught with guns, using Federal laws that require mandatory imprisonment. The first-year result was a 33% drop in homicides for the Richmond Metro area in a year where the national murder rate was climbing. This shows that enforcement works. According to Andrew McBride of the Richmond Department of Justice, these cases are as easy to prosecute as 'picking change up off the street.'"[167]

---

[165] Bureau of Justice Statistics, Federal Firearm Offenders and Background Checks for Firearm Transfers, June 4, 2000; U.S. Justice Department statistics, 1999.

[166] General Accounting Office report on the Implementation of NICS, February 2000.

[167] FBI Uniform Crime Statistics, 1999.

PART V

REGULATING GUN SALES AND TRANSFERS

CHAPTER 28

Waiting periods are ineffective in reducing crime.

Myth: Waiting periods prevent rash crimes and allow for a much-needed cooling off period.

Truth:

- "'Time-to-crime' is the period between a firearm's retail sale and law enforcement's recovery of the firearm in connection with a crime." "A Justice Department report states 'the recovery of a crime gun within 2 to 3 years after its initial purchase is considered a short time-to-crime and a significant trafficking indicator.'" By contrast, the ATF found that the average time-to-crime from between 2006 and 2010 was 10.5 years. Thus, waiting periods of a few days had no effect on the average crime gun.[168]
- A study compared the 32 states that implemented the Brady Act requirements of a background check and 5-day waiting period for handguns with the 18 states, and the District of Columbia, that already had such requirements in place: "Our analyses provide no evidence that implementation of

---

[168] CJ Ciaramella, *Slow and Not-So-Furious*, The Washington Free Beacon, Feb. 15, 2012, https://freebeacon.com/issues/slow-and-not-so-furious/.

the Brady Act was associated with a reduction in homicide rates."[169] "In particular, we find no differences in homicide or firearm homicide rates to adult victims in the 32 treatment states directly subject to the Brady Act provisions compared with the remaining control states."[170] Additionally, "we did not detect an association of the Brady Act with overall suicide rates."[171]

---

[169] Jens Ludwig & Philip J. Cook, *Homicide and Suicide Rates Associated With Implementation of the Brady Handgun Violence Prevention Act*, Journal of the American Medical Association, vol. 284, No. 5, at 588 (August 2, 2000), available at https://pdfs.semanticscholar.org/d6c7/359796f5a96874435a3c8443b623cd074254.pdf.

[170] Jens Ludwig & Philip J. Cook, *Homicide and Suicide Rates Associated With Implementation of the Brady Handgun Violence Prevention Act*, Journal of the American Medical Association, vol. 284, No. 5, at 588 (August 2, 2000), available at https://pdfs.semanticscholar.org/d6c7/359796f5a96874435a3c8443b623cd074254.pdf.

[171] Jens Ludwig & Philip J. Cook, *Homicide and Suicide Rates Associated With Implementation of the Brady Handgun Violence Prevention Act*, Journal of the American Medical Association, vol. 284, No. 5, at 590 (August 2, 2000), available at https://pdfs.semanticscholar.org/d6c7/359796f5a96874435a3c8443b623cd074254.pdf.

CHAPTER 29

Gun buybacks are typically ineffective.

Myth: Gun buybacks are a successful method of getting crime guns off the streets.

Truth:

- The National Institute of Justice divided crime prevention programs into categories of "What works," "What doesn't work," "What's promising," and What's unknown." "Gun buyback programs" were listed among the programs under "What doesn't work." This was because research showed that "Gun buyback programs operated without geographic limitations on the eligibility of people providing guns for money fail to reduce gun violence in cities."[172]
- Garen Wintemute, director of the Violence Prevention Research Program at the University of California at Davis, explained that "[b]uybacks remove generally no more than 1 or 2 percent of the guns estimated to be in the community." And further, "[t]he guns that are removed from the community do not resemble the guns used in crimes in that

---

[172] Lawrence W. Sherman, et al., *Preventing Crime: What Works, What Doesn't, What's Promising*, National Institute of Justice 8 (July 1998).

community. There has never been any effect on crime results seen."[173]

- The Washington Post pointed out that "[t]he guns of choice for young criminals . . . show up less often in buyback bins than in crime records. In a Boston study, 17 percent of buyback guns were semiautomatics, compared with 52 percent of guns confiscated from suspects younger than 22. In Sacramento, 35 percent of buyback guns were semiautomatics, compared with 57 percent of handguns seized by police in 1995."[174]
- Jon Vernick, co-director of Johns Hopkins Center for Gun Policy and Research, found that "there is no compelling evidence that gun buyback programs are an effective crime-fighting tool or that they reduce the rates of crime."[175]

---

173 Peter Slevin, *Buying Back Safe*r Streets, Washington Post, May 19, 2000, https://www.washingtonpost.com/archive/politics/2000/05/19/buying-back-safer-streets/afff27ef-7435-4ce1-aa86-f2aed8cba800/?noredirect=on&utm_term=.c81b1354890f.

174 Peter Slevin, *Buying Back Safe*r Streets, Washington Post, May 19, 2000, https://www.washingtonpost.com/archive/politics/2000/05/19/buying-back-safer-streets/afff27ef-7435-4ce1-aa86-f2aed8cba800/?noredirect=on&utm_term=.c81b1354890f.

175 Meghan E. Irons, *Success of gun buyback programs is debated*, Boston Globe, Feb. 13, 2014, https://www.bostonglobe.com/metro/2014/02/12/success-gun-buyback-program-debated/PsITjPCyPkrG9C7fFr979O/story.html.

- The Washington Post further acknowledged that "Studies also show that lawbreakers rarely surrender their weapons to buyback programs and that many people who do sell their guns have other firearms at home, or soon buy new ones."[176]
- "A report of Boston buyback programs published [in 2013] in the American Journal of Preventive Medicine noted: 'Licensed gun dealers from the suburbs used the event to clear their inventories of second-hand firearms that were worth less than the $50 incentive.'"[177]
- A study of a buyback program by the Sacramento Police Department found that "Forty three respondents [47% of participants] retained at least one gun in their household after participating in the program."[178]

---

[176] Peter Slevin, *Buying Back Safe*r Streets, WASHINGTON POST, May 19, 2000, https://www.washingtonpost.com/archive/politics/2000/05/19/buying-back-safer-streets/afff27ef-7435-4ce1-aa86-f2aed8cba800/?noredirect=on&utm_term=.c81b1354890f.

[177] Meghan E. Irons, *Success of gun buyback programs is debated*, BOSTON GLOBE, Feb. 13, 2014, https://www.bostonglobe.com/metro/2014/02/12/success-gun-buyback-program-debated/PsITjPCyPkrG9C7fFr979O/story.html.

[178] Michael P. Romero, et al., *Characteristics of a gun exchange program, and an assessment of potential benefits*, INJURY PREVENTION 208 (1998) https://www.ncbi.nlm.nih.gov/pmc/articles/PMC1730372/pdf/v004p00206.pdf.

CHAPTER 30

Background checks can sometimes have no effect in keeping guns out of criminals and the insane

Myth: Background checks will prevent insane people and criminals from getting their hand on guns, thereby reducing the number of gun deaths in the population.

Truth:

- Researchers at the Johns Hopkins Bloomberg School of Public Health and the University of California at Davis Violence Prevention Research Program conducted a joint study that found that California's much-publicized mandated background checks, which the state imposed on its citizens in 1991, had no impact on gun deaths. Researchers compared yearly gun suicide and homicide rates in California over the 10 years following the implementation of California's mandatory background check law in 1991 with 32 control states that did not have such laws. They found "no change in the rates of either cause of death from firearms through 2000."[179]

- 80% of police surveyed do not think that universal background checks would reduce crime.[180]

---

[179] Alvaro Castillo-Carniglia, et al., *California's comprehensive background check and misdemeanor violence prohibition policies and firearm mortality*, 30 ANNALS OF EPIDEMIOLOGY 50-56 (2019).

[180] PoliceOne, *Gun Policy & Law Enforcement*, March 2013.

CHAPTER 31

Imposing greater restrictions against firearm dealers will not reduce crime.

Myth: Putting greater restrictions on gun dealers will reduce guns on the street and, thus, crime.

Truth:

- Reforms of the Federal Firearms Licensing program, mainly focused on small volume retailers and traders, did not produce any significant results in reducing firearm crime rates.[181]

[181] Christopher Koper, Criminology & Public Policy, American Society of Criminology, March 2002.

PART VI

LICENSING AND REGISTRATION

CHAPTER 32

Gun registration is futile.

Myth: Gun registration will help police identify criminals.

Truth:

- John Lott emphasized how futile gun registration had been at solving crimes in an L.A. Times commentary in 2000: "In theory, if a gun is left at the scene of the crime, licensing and registration will allow a gun to be traced back to its owner. But, amazingly, despite police spending tens of thousands of man hours administering these laws in Hawaii (the one state with both rules), as well as in big urban areas with similar laws, such as Chicago and Washington, D.C., there is not even a single case where the laws have been instrumental in identifying someone who has committed a crime. The reason is simple. First, criminals very rarely leave their guns at the scene of the crime. Would-be criminals also virtually never get licenses or register their weapons."[182]
- Former San Jose police chief and fellow at Stanford University's Hoover Institution, Joseph McNamara, explained how gun registration can en-

[182] John R. Lott, Jr., *Gun Licensing Leads to Increased Crime, Lost Lives*, Los Angeles Times, Aug. 23, 2000, http://articles.latimes.com/2000/aug/23/local/me-8924.

danger lawful gun owners: "My research into more than a dozen raids that turned out badly is that ... the presence of a firearm wires officers into a much higher tendency to shoot . . . the presence of a legally possessed firearm bought to protect the home may get totally innocent people killed by the police who casually use SWAT for drug search warrants especially if they register."[183]

- Other law enforcement officers have expressed concerns about the futility of registration requirements. Ventura County Sheriff Bob Brooks complained that a registration and licensing law "significantly misses the mark because it diverts our attention from what should be our common goal: holding the true criminals accountable for the crimes they commit and getting them off the street."[184]

- Efforts to enforce registration requirements may be hampered by the privilege against self-incrimination protected by the Fifth Amendment. In, *Haynes v. United States*, the Supreme Court held "that a proper claim of the constitutional privilege against self-incrimination provides a full defense to prosecutions either for failure to register a firearm under [section] 5841 or for possession of an

---

183 Steven Greenhut, *California Gun Law Paves the Way for Confiscation*, REASON, Jan. 3, 2014, https://reason.com/archives/2014/01/03/california-gun-law-paves-the-way-for-con.

184 *When 'Gun Control' costs lives*, John Lott, Firing Line, September 2001.

unregistered firearm under [section] 5851" of the National Firearms Act.[185]

- When registration was required in Hawaii, Chicago and Washington DC, there was not a single case where registration was instrumental in identifying someone who committed a crime. This is not surprising, as criminals very rarely leave their guns at the scene of the crime, nor do they register their guns before committing a crime.[186]

---

185 390 U.S. 85, 100 (1968).

186 John Lott, *Gun Licensing Leads to Increased Crime, Lost Lives*, L.A. TIMES, Aug 23, 2000.

PART VII
EFFECT OF GUN CONTROL LAWS

CHAPTER 33

The Brady Bill did not cause a decrease in firearm homicides.

Myth: Gun registration will help police identify criminals.

Truth:

- Violent crime began to fall in 1991, and continued to fall for over two decades.[187] The Brady Bill became effective in 1994, yet the percentage of homicides committed with firearms remained consistent around 68% since before the Brady Bill was passed, all the way through the present day.[188] This indicates that the decrease in firearm-related homicides was part of an overall declining crime rate, and not a consequence of the Brady Bill.
- "The Brady Bill is not enforced. In 2006, of the nearly 70,000 Field Office referrals for instant background check violations (25,259 of which NICS identified as buyers with felony records),

---

[187] *See* FBI Uniform Crime Statistics 2011, Uniform Crime Reporting, Table 1, https://ucr.fbi.gov/crime-in-the-u.s/2011/crime-in-the-u.s.-2011/tables/table-1.

[188] *See* FBI Uniform Crime Statistics.

0.4% (273) were never charged with a crime and 0.1% (73) were convicted."[189]

- John Lott explained that:
- The Journal of the American Medical Assn. this month published an article showing that the Brady law produced no reduction in homicides or suicides. Other, more comprehensive research actually found that the waiting period in the Brady law slightly increased rape rates.
- The Clinton administration keeps issuing press releases boasting that violent crime rates have fallen since 1994, when the Brady law was adopted. Yet violent crime started falling in 1991. The Brady law did not apply to 18 states, but after 1994 their violent crime fell as quickly as other states.
- While still asserting that the law "must have some effect," U.S. Atty. Gen. Janet Reno was reduced this month to saying, "It might just take longer to measure [it]."[190]

---

[189] *Government, Laws, Social Costs*, Gun Facts, https://www.gunfacts.info/gun-control-myths/government-gun-laws-and-social-costs/.

[190] John R. Lott, Jr., *Gun Licensing Leads to Increased Crime, Lost Lives*, Los Angeles Times, Aug. 23, 2000, http://articles.latimes.com/2000/aug/23/local/me-8924 (brackets in the original).

CHAPTER 34

Gun control efforts have lost substantial support in recent decades.

Myth: Americans want more gun control.

Truth:

- In 1959, when Gallup first started asking Americans whether or not they believed that handguns should be banned, a staggering 60% of Americans agreed that handguns should be banned. In 2019, however, fewer than half that number—29%—agreed.[191]
- In 2015, Rasmussen found that "Americans are more supportive than they have been in the past of their constitutional right to bear arms. They remain closely divided over the need for more gun control but still tend to oppose it. Perhaps that's because just 38% think more gun control will keep guns out of the hands of people who shouldn't have them. Fifty-one percent (51%) think it will just make it harder for law-abiding citizens to buy a gun. Sizable majorities have said for years that

---

191 *Guns*, GALLUP, https://news.gallup.com/poll/1645/guns.aspx, (last visited August 7, 2018).

the government needs to enforce the gun laws already on the books instead."[192]

- A 2014 Pew Research Center poll found that "52% say it is more important to protect the right of Americans to own guns, while 46% say it is more important to control gun ownership."[193] In 2000, only 29% said protecting the right was more important, while 66% said control was more important. Thus, support for gun rights is growing, and support for control is shrinking.[194]
- A Pew Research Center poll from 2014 found that "Nearly six-in-ten Americans (57%) say gun ownership does more to protect people from becoming victims of crime, while 38% say it does more to endanger personal safety.[195]

---

[192] *What America Thinks: Is the Government After Your Guns?*, Rasmussen Reports, Dec. 15, 2015, http://www.rasmussenreports.com/public_content/videos/2015_12/what_america_thinks_is_the_government_after_your_guns.

[193] *Growing Public Support for Gun Rights*, Pew Research Center, Dec. 10, 2014, http://www.people-press.org/2014/12/10/growing-public-support-for-gun-rights/.

[194] *Continued Bipartisan Support for Expanded Background Checks on Gun Sales*, Pew Research Center, Aug. 13, 2015, https://www.pewresearch.org/wp-content/uploads/sites/4/2015/08/08-13-15-Guns-release.pdf.

[195] *Growing Public Support for Gun Rights*, Pew Research Center, Dec. 10, 2014, http://www.people-press.org/2014/12/10/growing-public-support-for-gun-rights/.

- In 2014, Gallup reported that "The percentage of Americans who believe having a gun in the house makes it a safer place to be (63%) has nearly doubled since 2000, when about one in three agreed with this. Three in 10 Americans say having a gun in the house makes it a more dangerous place."[196]
- "A [2015] Rasmussen Reports national telephone survey [found] that 63% of Americans with a gun in their household f[elt] safer because someone in that household owns a gun. Just two percent (2%) sa[id] having a gun in the house ma[de]them feel less safe, while 32% sa[id] it ha[d] no impact on their personal safety."[197]

---

[196] Justin McCarthy, *More Than Six in 10 Americans Say Guns Make Homes Safer*, Gallup, Nov. 7, 2014, https://news.gallup.com/poll/179213/six-americans-say-guns-homes-safer.aspx.

[197] *Gun Owners Feel Safer*, Rasmussen Reports, Dec. 10, 2015, http://www.rasmussenreports.com/public_content/politics/current_events/gun_control/gun_owners_feel_safer.

- Another 2015 "Rasmussen Reports national telephone survey f[ound] that just 22% of [l]ikely U.S. Voters would feel safer living in a neighborhood where nobody was allowed to own a gun over one where they could have a gun for their own protection. Sixty-eight percent (68%) would feel safer in a neighborhood where guns are allowed, while 10% are not sure."[198]

---

[198] *Americans Prefer Living in Neighborhoods With Guns*, RASMUSSEN REPORTS, June 12, 2015, HTTP://WWW.RASMUSSENREPORTS.COM/PUBLIC_CONTENT/POLITICS/CURRENT_EVENTS/GUN_CONTROL/AMERICANS_PREFER_LIVING_IN_NEIGHBORHOODS_WITH_GUNS.

CHAPTER 35

The majority of Americans think that having a gun in the home makes it safer.

Myth: Most Americans think that guns in the home are dangerous.

Truth:

- A Gallup poll found that 63% of Americans believe that having a firearm in the home makes it safer.[199]
- 68% of Americans would feel safer living in a neighborhood where they are allowed to own a gun than a neighborhood where one could have a gun for their own protection.[200]

---

199 Gallup, *More Than Six in Ten Americans Say Guns Make Home Safer,* November 2014.

200 Rasmussen Reports, June 2015.

CHAPTER 36

Foreign countries with strict gun control laws do not necessarily have less crime than the United States.

Myth: Foreign countries with stricter gun control laws than the United States have less crime than the United States.

Truth:

- Countries with the strictest gun-control laws also tend to have the highest homicide rates.[201]
- The United States is not in the top 100 countries for homicides. The top ten countries all have near or total firearm bans.[202]

---

201 Jeffery A. Miron, *Violence, Guns and Drugs: A Cross-Country Analysis*, Department of Economics, Boston University, JOURNAL OF LAW & ECONOMICS, University of Chicago Press, October 2001.

202 United Nations Office on Drugs and Crime, 2010.

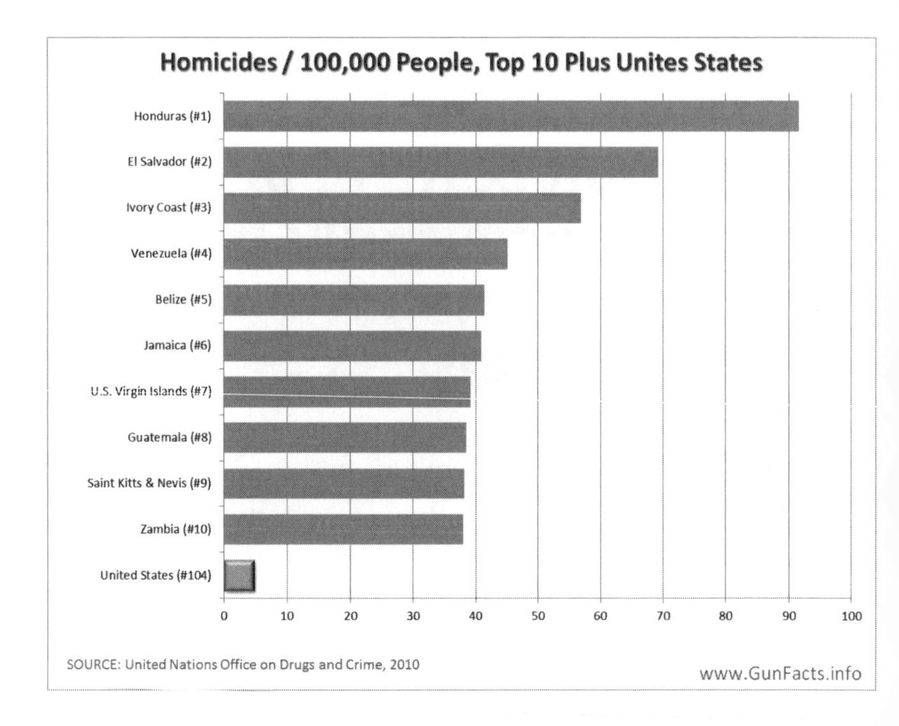

- Thanks in large part to the 2.5 million annual defense gun uses, the United States has a violent crime rate that is lower than 12 of 17 industrialized, high-income countries.[203]
- "… [T]he major surveys completed in the past 20 years or more provides no evidence of any relationship between the total number of legally held firearms in society and the rate of armed crime. Nor is there a relationship between the severity of

203 *See* Dutch Ministry of Justice, *Criminal Victimization in Seventeen Industrialized Countries*, 2001; *see also* Gary Kleck, *Targeting Guns*, Aldine Transaction, 1997.

controls imposed in various countries or the mass of bureaucracy involved with many control systems with the apparent ease of access to firearms by criminals and terrorists."[204]

- When Great Britain decided to implement severe gun control measures, thereby decreasing the availability of guns to its citizens, homicide and firearm homicide rates shot up, even though most developed countries in Europe at that time experienced a downward trend in those rates. Likewise, the homicide rates in Ireland shot up in the years immediately following Ireland's 1972 gun confiscation legislation. And Australia's armed and unarmed robbery rates both increased significantly in the five years following Australia's National Firearms Act.[205]

- Firearms are much more available to Americans than to Brits, who have some of the strictest gun control laws in the world, but the violent crime rates for homicide, burglary, rape, and aggravated assault are much lower in America than in Great Britain. Also, approximately 60% of burglaries in Great Britain occur while citizens are at home, compared to just 13% in America. British burglars admit that they are more likely to target occupied residences because they are more likely to find

---

[204] Colin Greenwood, *Minutes of Evidence*, Select Committee on Northern Ireland Affairs, January 29, 2003.

[205] *See* John Lott, THE WAR ON GUNS: ARMING YOURSELF AGAINST GUN CONTROL LIES (2016).

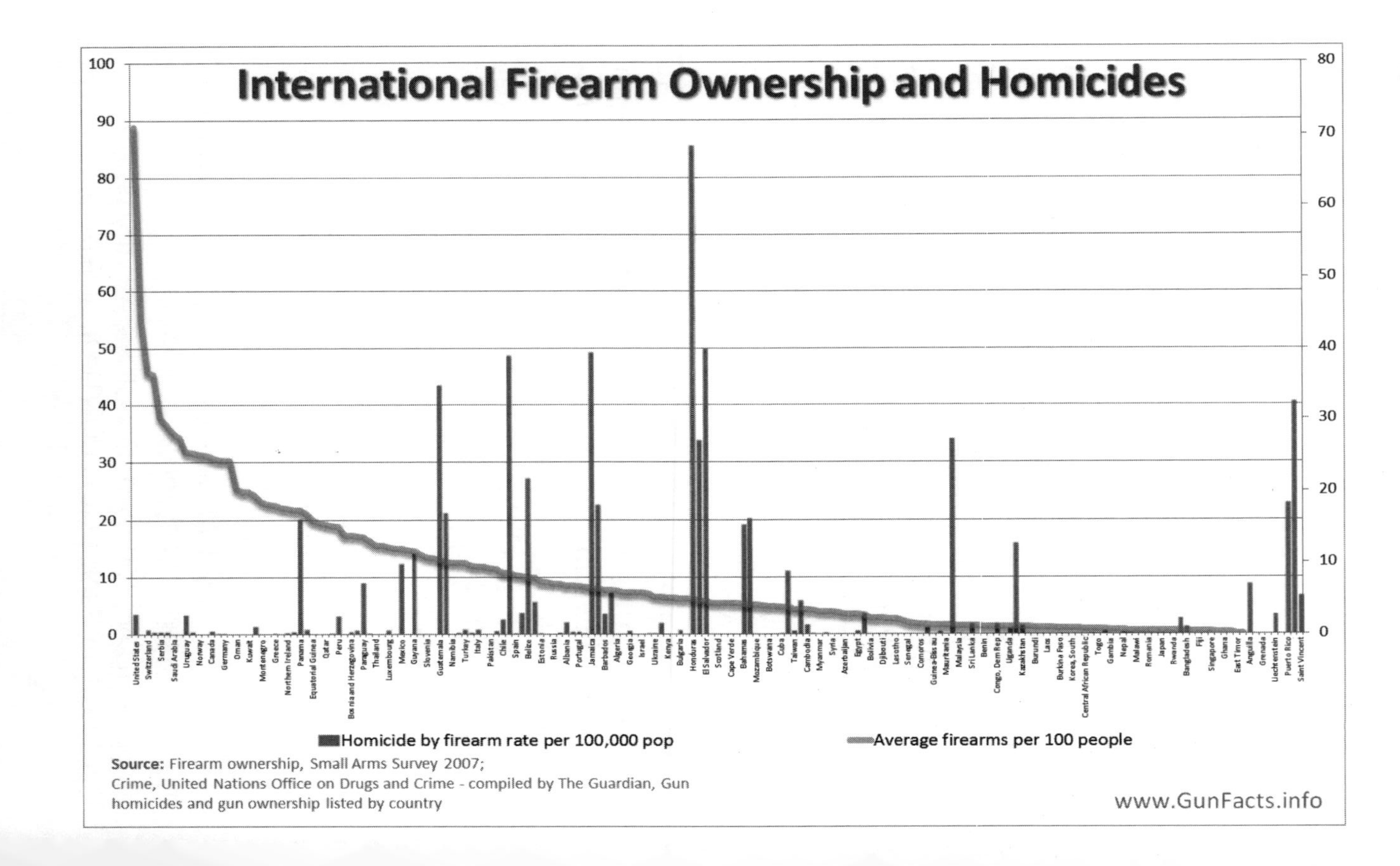
International Firearm Ownership and Homicides
100
90
80
70
60
50
40
30
20
10
0
80
70
60
50
40
30
20
10
0
United States
Switzerland
Serbia
Saudi Arabia
Uruguay
Norway
Canada
Germany
Oman
Kuwait
Montenegro
Greece
Northern Ireland
Panama
Equatorial Guinea
Qatar
Peru
Bosnia and Herzegovina
Paraguay
Thailand
Luxembourg
Mexico
Guyana
Slovenia
Guatemala
Namibia
Turkey
Italy
Pakistan
Chile
Spain
Belize
Estonia
Russia
Albania
Portugal
Jamaica
Barbados
Algeria
Georgia
Israel
Ukraine
Kenya
Bulgaria
Honduras
El Salvador
Scotland
Cape Verde
Bahamas
Mozambique
Botswana
Cuba
Taiwan
Cambodia
Myanmar
Syria
Azerbaijan
Egypt
Bolivia
Djibouti
Lesotho
Senegal
Comoros
Guinea-Bissau
Mauritania
Malaysia
Sri Lanka
Benin
Congo, Dem Rep
Uganda
Kazakhstan
Burundi
Laos
Burkina Faso
Korea, South
Central African Republic
Togo
Gambia
Nepal
Malawi
Romania
Japan
Rwanda
Bangladesh
Fiji
Singapore
Ghana
East Timor
Anguilla
Grenada
Liechtenstein
Puerto Rico
Saint Vincent
Homicide by firearm rate per 100,000 pop
Average firearms per 100 people
Source: Firearm ownership, Small Arms Survey 2007;
Crime, United Nations Office on Drugs and Crime - compiled by The Guardian, Gun homicides and gun ownership listed by country
www.GunFacts.info

wallets and purses there and, perhaps, less likely to find an armed resident ready to engage in self-defense.[206]

- One study of Canadian firearms law and homicide rates spanning 34 years "failed to demonstrate a beneficial association between legislation and fire-arm homicide rates" for three major gun control bills.[207]
- The United States is not the source of 90% of drug syndicate guns in Mexico, contrary to public be-lief. The original 90% number came from BAFTE's statement of the number of firearms successfully traced, not the total number of firearms criminally used. For example, in 2007-2008, Mexican officials recovered approximately 29,000 firearms from crime scenes and asked for BATFE traces of 11,000. Of those, the BATFE could trace roughly 6,000. Of those 6,000, 5,114 were confirmed to have come from the United States. Consequently, 83% of the crime guns recovered in Mexico have not been or cannot be traced to America.[208]

---

[206] The Heritage Foundation, *Here Are 8 Stubborn Facts on Gun Violence in America* (2018).

[207] Caillin Langmann, *Canadian Firearms Legislation and Effects on Homicide 1974 to 2008*, JOURNAL OF INTERPERSONAL VIOLENCE, September 30, 2011.

[208] Fox News, *The Myth of 90 Percent: BATFE data distilled by William La Jeunesse and Maxim Lott*, April 2, 2009.

PART VIII
GUN VIOLENCE

CHAPTER 37

Lawfully purchased guns are rarely used in crimes.

Myth: Lawfully purchased guns frequently turn into crime guns.

Truth:

- The Cincinnati Initiative to Reduce Violence determined that "approximately 74% of the homicides [committed in Cincinnati from June 8, 2006 through June 6, 2007] involved a victim and/or an offender known by law enforcement to be associated with a violent street group."[209] This "confirms that a very small segment of the total city population (less than 1%) is responsible for the majority of the violence (74% of homicides)."[210]
- According to the National Gang Intelligence Center, "Gangs are responsible for an average of 48

---

[209] Robin S. Engel, *Implementation of the Cincinnati Initiative to Reduce Violence: Year 1 Report* at 9, University of Cincinnati Policing Institute, (Apr. 14, 2008), https://www.cincinnati-oh.gov/police/linkservid/A98E79DE-B015-4635-9E66EDBBC4824C7D/showMeta/0/.

[210] Robin S. Engel, *Implementation of the Cincinnati Initiative to Reduce Violence: Year 1 Report* at 11, University of Cincinnati Policing Institute (Apr. 14, 2008), https://www.cincinnati-oh.gov/police/linkservid/A98E79DE-B015-4635-9E66EDBBC4824C7D/showMeta/0/.

percent of violent crime in most jurisdictions and up to 90 percent in several others."[211] And guns are used in 92% of gang related homicides.[212]

- "[Philip] Cook and colleagues Susan Parker and Harold Pollack at the University of Chicago interviewed 99 inmates of the Cook County Jail in Chicago . . . of the 70 inmates who had possessed a firearm, only 2, or 2.9 percent, had bought it at a gun store. The report found that percentage was in line with the findings of the Chicago Police Department when it traced weapons seized from suspected gang members."[213]

---

[211] FBI *2011 National Gang Threat Assessment – Emerging Trends*, https://www.fbi.gov/stats-services/publications/2011-national-gang-threat-assessment.

[212] U.S. Department of Justice, Bureau of Justice Statistics, *Homicide Trends in the United States* 26 (Nov. 2011), https://www.bjs.gov/content/pub/pdf/htus8008.pdf.

[213] Jon Greenberg, *MSNBC's Joe Scarborough: Tiny fraction of crimes committed with legal guns*, PolitiFact, Oct. 5, 2015, https://www.politifact.com/punditfact/statements/2015/oct/05/joe-scarborough/msnbcs-joe-scarborough-tiny-fraction-crimes-commit/ (citing Philip J. Cook, *Sources of guns to dangerous people: What we learn by asking them*, Preventative Medicine, vol. 79, 28–36 (Oct. 2015), available at https://www.sciencedirect.com/science/article/pii/S0091743515001486).

- "An estimated 500,000 to 1.4 million firearms are stolen annually. According to sociologist Gary Kleck:

  > Even if one could completely eliminate all voluntary transfers of guns to criminals, including lawful or unlawful transfers, involving either licensed dealers or private citizens, and even if police could completely confiscate all firearms from all criminals each year, a single year's worth of gun thefts alone would be more than sufficient to rearm all gun criminals and easily supply the entire set of guns needed to commit the current number of gun crimes."[214]

- A Special Report from the U.S. Department of Justice found that an average of 102,590 firearms were stolen from households each year from 2003 to 2007.[215] (While this number is lower than most other estimates, it is limited to only households.)

---

[214] James B. Jacobs, CAN GUN CONTROL WORK? 102 (2004).

[215] Shannan M. Catalano, Bureau of Justice Statistics: *Victimization During Household Burglary* 7 (2010), available at https://www.bjs.gov/content/pub/pdf/vdhb.pdf.

CHAPTER 38

The availability of guns does not increase crime.

Myth: The easier guns are for citizens to access, the more crime there is.

Truth:

- As the chart from Gun Facts (next page) shows, while America's handgun supply has steadily increased in recent decades, the homicide rate has dropped significantly, and the suicide rate has remained essentially the same. This casts doubt on any claim that handguns cause more homicides and suicides.[216]
- In fact, as more and more Americans have lawful access to guns, America is on a trend of becoming even safer. According to the National Crime Victimization Survey, violent crime has been declining steadily since the early 1990's. According to Pew Research, the 2011 homicide rate was almost half of the rate in 1991, the 2013 gun-related death rate was half of that in 1993, and the number of non-fatal firearm crimes committed in 2011 was one-sixth the number committed in 1993.

---

216 *Availability of Guns*, GUN FACTS, http://www.gunfacts.info/gun-control-myths/availability-of-guns/.

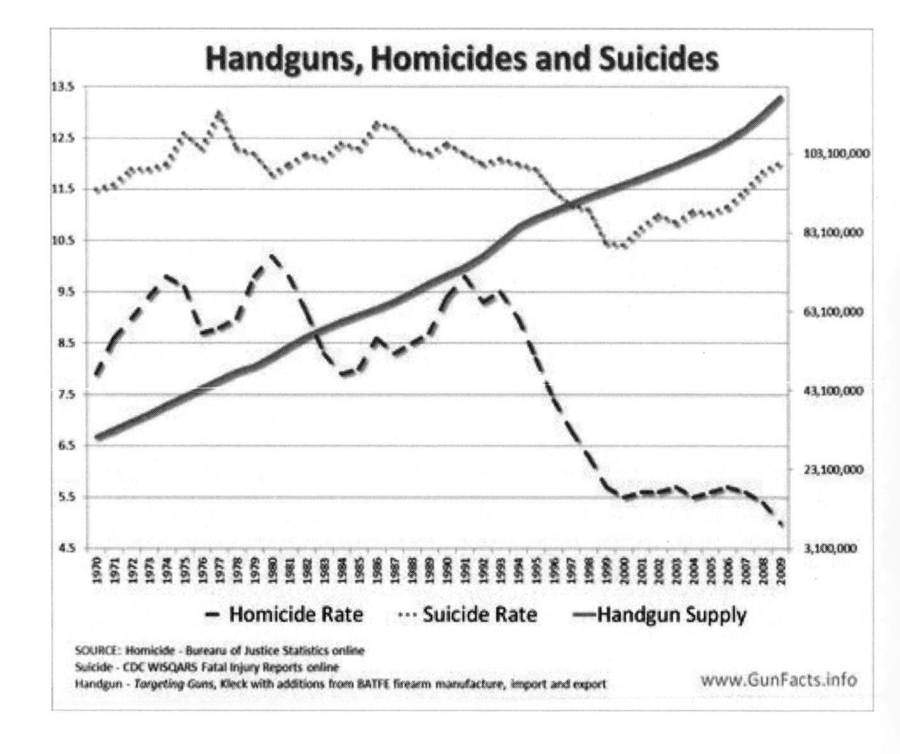

- Gun violence does not even make the top ten list of public health problems in the United States put out by the Centers for Disease Control.[217]
- "[A] 1986 survey found that five out of six prison inmates reported obtaining their handguns in the secondary market or by theft, and that the criminal handgun market is overwhelmingly dominated

217 *See* Centers for Disease Control, *Prevention Status Report* (2020).

by informal transactions and theft as mechanisms of supply."[218]

- Even though the rate of gun ownership is higher in rural areas than in urban areas, rural areas still experience much lower murder rates.[219]
- States ranked by The Brady Campaign Against Gun Violence to have less restrictive gun laws, meaning that guns are more available to their citizens (e.g., Vermont, Idaho, New Hampshire, and Oregon) have some of the lowest homicide rates in the nation. Meanwhile, states ranked by The Brady Campaign Against Gun Violence as having more restrictive gun laws, meaning that guns are less available to their citizens (e.g., Illinois and Maryland), have some of the nation's highest homicide rates.[220]
- According to sociologists Joseph F. Sheley's and James D. Wright's study of juvenile felons and a control group of inner-city youths, 54% of the inmates and 37% of the control group indicated that they could easily obtain a handgun 'off the street.' An even higher percentage reported that they could get a handgun from a friend or family member (45% and 53% respectively). Of the inmates surveyed, 83% owned a gun at the time of

---

[218] James B. Jacobs, CAN GUN CONTROL WORK? 101-02 (2004).

[219] The Heritage Foundation, *Here Are 8 Stubborn Facts on Gun Violence in America* (2018).

[220] The Heritage Foundation, *Here Are 8 Stubborn Facts on Gun Violence in America* (2018).

arrest, while 22% of the control group admitted to owning a gun at the time of the survey. Sheley and Wright found that the leading sources of handguns were (1) borrowing from a family member or friend (45% of juvenile inmates; 53% of controls); (2) buying 'off the street' (54% of inmates; 37% of controls); (3) buying from a family member or friend (36% of inmates; 35% of controls); (4) buying from a drug dealer or addict (36% of inmates; 22% controls); (5) buying from a gun shop (12% of inmates; 28% of controls); and (6) theft (17% of inmates; 8% of controls). . . . Sheley and Wright concluded that unregulated purchases and trades between private parties subverts legal measures, designed to prevent dangerous individuals from obtaining guns."[221]

- Gun Facts points out that, "Most violent crime is caused by a small minority of repeat offenders. One California study found that 3.8% of a group of males born in 1956 were responsible for 55.5% of all serious felonies. 75-80% of murder arrestees have prior arrests for a violent (including non-fatal) felony or burglary. On average, they have about four felony arrests and one felony conviction."[222]
- A national survey by the Department of Justice in 1991 found that "of all persons who were arrested

---

221 James B. Jacobs, Can Gun Control Work? 102 (2004).

222 *The Prevalence and Incidence of Arrest Among Adult Males in California*, Robert Tillman, prepared for California Department of Justice, Bureau of Criminal Statistics and Special Services, Sacramento, California, 1987.

for the murder of a law enforcement officer from 1988 to 1992, 22% were on probation or parole at the time of the killing. Similarly, of arrested murderers who were convicted, acquitted, or whose cases were otherwise disposed in 1992 in urban courts, 38% were on probation, on parole, on pretrial release, or in some other criminal justice status at the time of the murder."[223]

- A Department of Justice survey of felony defendants in the 75 largest counties in the United States between 1990 to 2009 found:

  - 66% of murder defendants had an arrest record at the time they were arrested.[224] 58% had been

---

[223] Robert L. Cohen, *Probation and Parole Violators in State Prison, 1991*, U.S. Justice Department: Bureau of Justice Statistics 9 (Aug. 1995), https://www.bjs.gov/content/pub/pdf/PPVSP91.PDF.

[224] Brian A. Reaves, *Felony Defendants in Large Urban Counties, 2009 – Statistical Tables*, U.S. Justice Department: Bureau of Justice Statistics 10 (Dec. 2013), https://www.bjs.gov/content/pub/pdf/fdluc09.pdf.

arrested for a felony.[225] 33% had 10 or more prior charges.[226] 20% had 10 or more felony charges.[227]

- 48% had prior convictions. 37% had multiple prior convictions.[228] 40% were convicted felons. And 27% had multiple felony convictions.[229]
- 17% were on probation or parole at the time they were arrested for murder.[230]

---

225 Brian A. Reaves, *Felony Defendants in Large Urban Counties, 2009 – Statistical Tables,* U.S. Justice Department: Bureau of Justice Statistics 11 (Dec. 2013), https://www.bjs.gov/content/pub/pdf/fdluc09.pdf.

226 Brian A. Reaves, *Felony Defendants in Large Urban Counties, 2009 – Statistical Tables,* U.S. Justice Department: Bureau of Justice Statistics 10 (Dec. 2013), https://www.bjs.gov/content/pub/pdf/fdluc09.pdf.

227 Brian A. Reaves, *Felony Defendants in Large Urban Counties, 2009 – Statistical Tables,* U.S. Justice Department: Bureau of Justice Statistics 11 (Dec. 2013), https://www.bjs.gov/content/pub/pdf/fdluc09.pdf.

228 Brian A. Reaves, *Felony Defendants in Large Urban Counties, 2009 – Statistical Tables,* U.S. Justice Department: Bureau of Justice Statistics 12 (Dec. 2013), https://www.bjs.gov/content/pub/pdf/fdluc09.pdf.

229 Brian A. Reaves, *Felony Defendants in Large Urban Counties, 2009 – Statistical Tables,* U.S. Justice Department: Bureau of Justice Statistics 13 (Dec. 2013), https://www.bjs.gov/content/pub/pdf/fdluc09.pdf.

230 Brian A. Reaves, *Felony Defendants in Large Urban Counties, 2009 – Statistical Tables,* U.S. Justice Department: Bureau of Justice Statistics 9 (Dec. 2013), https://www.bjs.gov/content/pub/pdf/fdluc09.pdf.

CHAPTER 39

The availability of guns does not increase suicides.

Myth: The easier guns are for citizens to access, the more suicide occurrences there are.

Truth:

- The following charts, from Gun Facts, compare suicide rate and gun ownership by country. They reveal no apparent relationship between the availability of firearms and suicides.[231]

[231] *Availability of Guns*, GUN FACTS, http://www.gunfacts.info/gun-control-myths/availability-of-guns/.

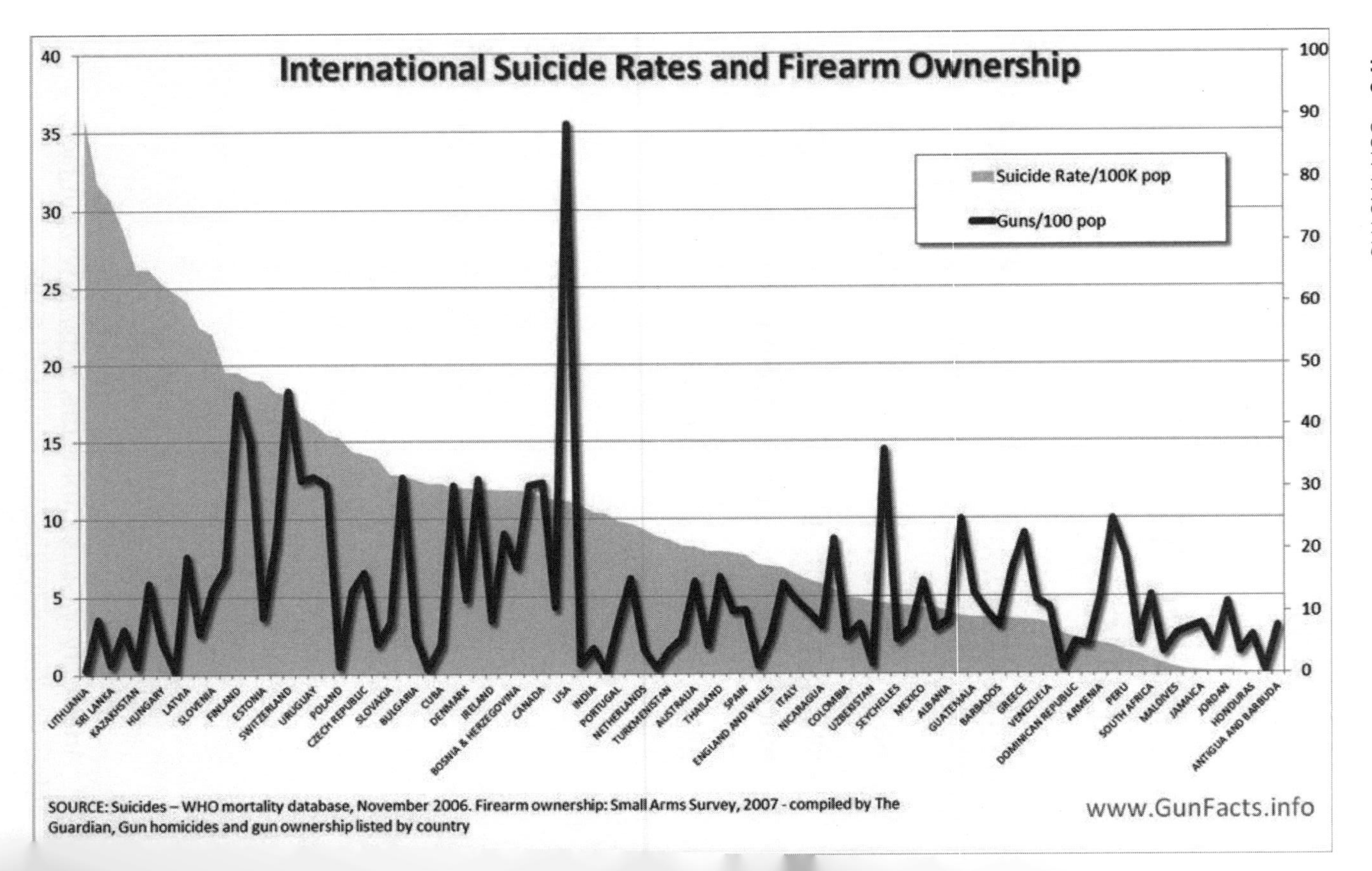
International Suicide Rates and Firearm Ownership
Suicide Rate/100K pop
Guns/100 pop
40
35
30
25
20
15
10
5
0
100
90
80
70
60
50
40
30
20
10
0
LITHUANIA
SRI LANKA
KAZAKHSTAN
HUNGARY
LATVIA
SLOVENIA
FINLAND
ESTONIA
SWITZERLAND
URUGUAY
POLAND
CZECH REPUBLIC
SLOVAKIA
BULGARIA
CUBA
DENMARK
IRELAND
BOSNIA & HERZEGOVINA
CANADA
USA
INDIA
PORTUGAL
NETHERLANDS
TURKMENISTAN
AUSTRALIA
THAILAND
SPAIN
ENGLAND AND WALES
ITALY
NICARAGUA
COLOMBIA
UZBEKISTAN
SEYCHELLES
MEXICO
ALBANIA
GUATEMALA
BARBADOS
GREECE
VENEZUELA
DOMINICAN REPUBLIC
ARMENIA
PERU
SOUTH AFRICA
MALDIVES
JAMAICA
JORDAN
HONDURAS
ANTIGUA AND BARBUDA
SOURCE: Suicides – WHO mortality database, November 2006. Firearm ownership: Small Arms Survey, 2007 - compiled by The Guardian, Gun homicides and gun ownership listed by country
www.GunFacts.info

- This chart, also from Gun Facts, compares suicide rate and gun ownership in the United States. It similarly reveals no apparent relationship between the availability of firearms and suicides.[232] Note that the United States and Canada have nearly identical suicide rates, but Canada has significantly lower gun ownership.[233]

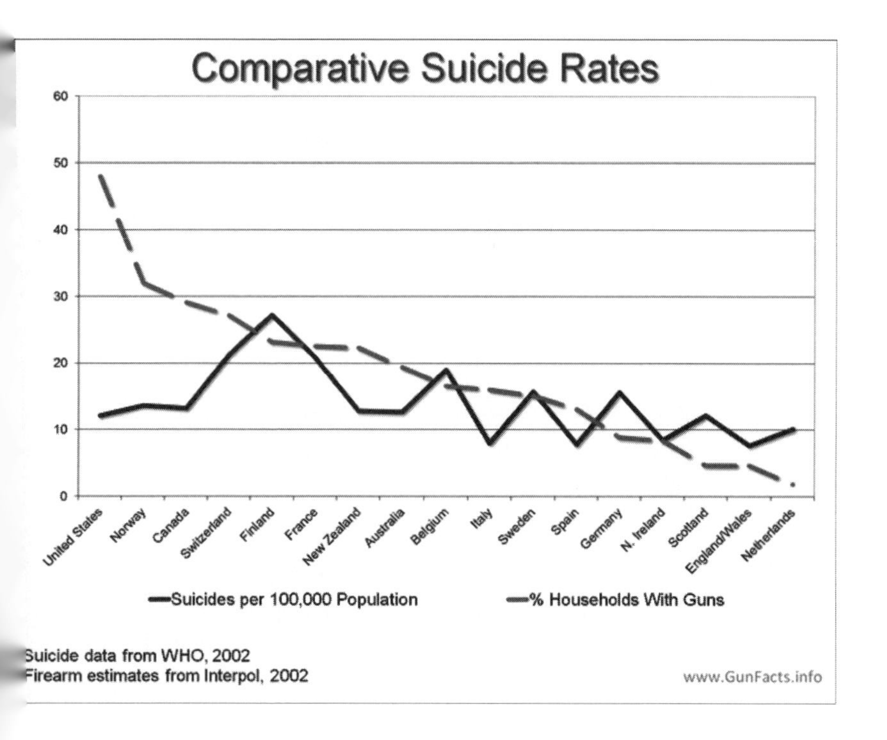

232 *Availability of Guns*, Gun Facts, http://www.gunfacts.info/gun-control-myths/availability-of-guns/.

233 *Availability of Guns*, Gun Facts, http://www.gunfacts.info/gun-control-myths/availability-of-guns/.

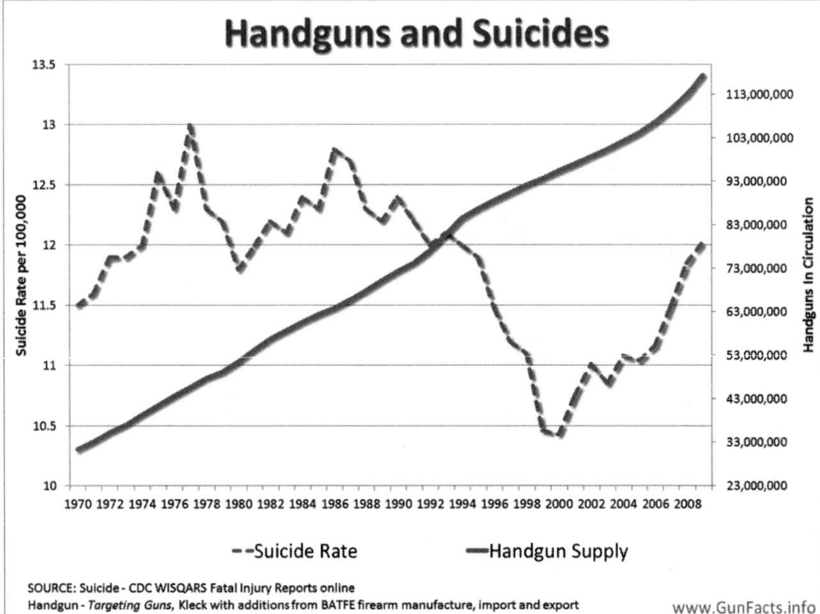
Handguns and Suicides
13.5
13
12.5
12
11.5
11
10.5
10
Suicide Rate per 100,000
113,000,000
103,000,000
93,000,000
83,000,000
73,000,000
63,000,000
53,000,000
43,000,000
33,000,000
23,000,000
Handguns In Circulation
1970 1972 1974 1976 1978 1980 1982 1984 1986 1988 1990 1992 1994 1996 1998 2000 2002 2004 2006 2008
Suicide Rate
Handgun Supply
SOURCE: Suicide - CDC WISQARS Fatal Injury Reports online
Handgun - Targeting Guns, Kleck with additions from BATFE firearm manufacture, import and export
www.GunFacts.info

CHAPTER 40

The availability of guns does not increase the chances of police officers getting killed on duty.

Myth: In states with more guns, more police officers are killed while on duty.

Truth:

- Police homicide rates are so low that any study claiming that more officers are killed on duty in states with more guns is riddled with statistical inaccuracies due to the rareness of such killings.[234] For example, only 47 officers were killed with guns in 2014 (not including firearm accidents).[235] So the researchers were trying to compare police homicides for each state when there was less than one such homicide per state on average.[236]

---

234 Swedler, Simmons, Dominici, and Hemenway,*Firearm Prevalence and Homicides of Law Enforcement Officers in the United States*, AMERICAN JOURNAL OF PUBLIC HEALTH, October 2015.

235 See *Officer Down Memorial Page*, https://www.odmp.org/.

236

CHAPTER 41

Handguns are not 43 times more likely to kill a family member than a criminal.

Myth: Handguns are 43 times more likely to kill a family member than a criminal.

Truth:

- Of the 43-to-1 figure, 37 (86%) were suicides. Others were the deaths of criminals.[237]
- "Now, how about the self-defense homicides, which Kellermann and Reay found to be so rare? Well, the reason that they found such a low total was that they excluded many cases of lawful self-defense. Kellermann and Reay did not count in the self-defense total of any of the cases where a person who had shot an attacker was acquitted on grounds of self-defense, or cases where a conviction was reversed on appeal on grounds related to self-defense. Yet 40% of women who appeal their

[237] Arthur L. Kellermann and Donald T. Reay, *Protection or Peril?: An Analysis of Firearm-Related Deaths in the Home*, New England Journal of Medicine, 1557–60 (1986).

murder convictions have the conviction reversed on appeal."[238]

- "Finally, Kellermann and Reay ignore the most important factor of all in assessing the risks of gun ownership: whose home the gun is in. You don't need a medical researcher to tell you that guns can be misused when in the homes of persons with mental illness related to violence; or in the homes of persons prone to self-destructive, reckless behavior; or in the homes of persons with arrest records for violent felonies; or in the homes where the police have had to intervene to deal with domestic violence. These are the homes from which the vast majority of handgun fatalities come."[239]

---

[238] David Kopel, *The Fallacy of "43 to 1"*, NATIONAL REVIEW ONLINE, Jan. 31, 2001, available at http://davekopel.org/NRO/2001/The-Fallacy-of-43-to-1.htm.

[239] David Kopel, *The Fallacy of "43 to 1"*, NATIONAL REVIEW ONLINE, Jan. 31, 2001, available at http://davekopel.org/NRO/2001/The-Fallacy-of-43-to-1.htm.

CHAPTER 42

There is no "gun show loophole" that allows criminals to get guns.

Myth: The "gun show loophole" is a substantial source of crime guns.

Truth:

- A government survey in 1991 found that among the 16% of state inmates that were armed during the commission of their crime, a mere 0.6% acquired their firearm from a gun show. Similarly, the survey found that in 1997, gun shows were the source of 0.7% of crime guns among the 18% of state inmates that committed their crime armed.[240]
- The Bureau of Justice Statistics releases conducted a decadal analysis of gun and crime, and in *Firearm Violence, 1993-2011*, it tallied the sources from where crime guns were obtained. Gun shows are only 0.8% of the problem.[241]

---

[240] U.S. Department of Justice: Bureau of Justice Statistics, *Firearm Use by Offenders* 1 (2001), https://www.bjs.gov/content/pub/pdf/fuo.pdf.

[241] Bureau of Justice Statistics, *Firearm Violence, 1993-2011.*

TABLE 14
Source of firearms possessed by state prison inmates at time of offense, 1997 and 2004

	Percent of state prison inmates	
Source of firearm	1997	2004
Total	100%	100%
Purchased or traded from—	14.0%	11.3%
Retail store	8.2	7.3
Pawnshop	4.0	2.6
Flea market	1.0	0.6
Gun show	0.8	0.8
Family or friend	40.1%	37.4%
Purchased or traded	12.6	12.2
Rented or borrowed	18.9	14.1
Other	8.5	11.1
Street/illegal source	37.3%	40.0%
Theft or burglary	9.1	7.5
Drug dealer/off street	20.3	25.2
Fence/black market	8.0	7.4
Other	8.7%	11.2%

- Most crime guns were acquired through a street/illegal source (39.2% in 1997 and 40.8% in 1991) or from friends or family members (39.6% in 1997 and 33.8% in 1991).[242]

- "Beginning in 1995, [the National Institute of Justice's Drug Use Forecasting] began asking arrestees about guns with a special questionnaire. The DUF gun data, for example, showed that most

[242] U.S. Department of Justice: Bureau of Justice Statistics, *Firearm Use by Offenders* 1 (2001), https://www.bjs.gov/content/pub/pdf/fuo.pdf.

arrestees reported obtaining their weapons from street sources. About 35 percent of handguns were obtained from the streets, about 23 percent from family or friends, 20 percent from gun stores, and 9 percent from pawnshops. Less than 1 percent reported obtaining handguns from victims or from theft, and less than 2 percent reported obtaining them from a gun show."[243]

- Reporting on an FBI study of shootings of police officers, Force Science News (of the Force Science Institute) explained: "Predominately handguns were used in the assaults on officers and all but one were obtained illegally, usually in street transactions or in thefts. In contrast to media myth, none of the firearms in the study was obtained from gun shows."[244]

---

[243] Pamela K. Lattimore, et al., *Homicides in Eight U.S. Cities: Trends, Context, and Policy Implications*, U.S. Department of Justice: National Institute of Justice 99 (Dec. 1997), https://www.ncjrs.gov/pdffiles1/ondcp/homicide_trends.pdf.

[244] *Force Science News #62*, Force Science News, Dec. 28, 2006, http://www.forcesciencenews.com/home/detail.html?serial=62.

CHAPTER 43

More regulation of gun shows will not necessarily reduce "straw sales."

Myth: More regulation of gun shows will reduce "straw sales."

Truth:

- This myth stems mainly from a study by Dr. Garen Wintemute that had no scientific basis for determining what sales at a gun show constitutes a "straw sale." Behaviors that Dr. Wintemute cited as "clear evidence" of a straw purchase were merely observational and were more likely instances of more experienced acquaintances helping someone make a purchase decision. Further, there were no attempts to verify that the sales in question were indeed straw sales.[245]

---

[245] *See* Garen J. Wintemute, *Gun Shows Across a Multistate American Gun Market*, British Medical Journal,, 2007.

CHAPTER 44

The benefits of defensive gun use exceed the social costs of firearms crimes.

Myth: The social costs of gun crimes justify strict gun restrictions.

Truth:

- A study by **H. Sterling Burnett, a** Senior Policy Analyst at the National Center for Policy Analysis, determined that "Even using the statistics most favorable to proponents of lawsuits against the gun industry, the benefits to society of defensive gun use are greater than the costs of firearm crimes by at least $90.7 million and perhaps as much as $3.5 billion per year. Using more reasonable estimates, the benefits of defensive gun use exceed the costs of firearm crimes by as much as $38.9 billion - an amount equal to about $400 per year for every household in America." Factors that affect the different estimates include lost work time, medical expenses, lost property, police work, and legal expenses.[246]

---

[246] H. Sterling Burnett, *Suing Gun Manufacturers: Hazardous to Our Health,* NATIONAL CENTER FOR POLICY ANALYSIS, No. 223, at 1 (Mar. 1, 1999), available at http://www.ncpathinktank.org/pub/st223.

PART IX
THE GUN CONTROL LOBBY'S AGENDA

CHAPTER 45

People *do* want to take your guns.

Myth: "Nobody wants to take your guns."[247]

Truth:

- Eugene Volokh, Professor of Law at UCLA Law School, compiled the following list of gun control proponents favoring a ban:[248]
  - **Charles Krauthammer**: "In fact, the assault weapons ban will have no significant effect either on the crime rate or on personal security. Nonetheless, it is a good idea . . . Its only real justification is not to reduce crime but to desensitize the public to the regulation of weapons in preparation for their ultimate confiscation . . . De-escalation begins with a change in mentality. And that change in mentality starts with the symbolic yielding of certain types of weapons. The real steps, like the banning of handguns,

[247] "No one is seriously proposing to ban or confiscate all guns. You hear that only from the gun lobby itself, which whistles up this bogeyman whenever some reasonable regulation is proposed." Martin Dyckman, associate editor of the St. Petersburg Times (Dec. 12, 1993, at 3D).

[248] Eugene Volokh, *Calls for Gun Bans*, GUNSCHOLAR.COM, http://gunscholar.com/gunban.htm#politicians.

will never occur unless this one is taken first, and even then not for decades."[249]

- **Pete Shields (founder of Handgun Control, Inc.)**: "We're going to have to take one step at a time, and the first step is necessarily -- given the political realities -- going to be very modest. . . . [W]e'll have to start working again to strengthen that law, and then again to strengthen the next law, and maybe again and again. Right now, though, we'd be satisfied not with half a loaf but with a slice. Our ultimate goal -- total control of handguns in the United States -- is going to take time. . . . The first problem is to slow down the number of handguns being produced and sold in this country. The second problem is to get handguns registered. The final problem is to make possession of all handguns and all handgun ammunition-except for the military, police, licensed security guards, licensed sporting clubs, and licensed gun collectors-totally illegal."[250]

- **Rep. William L. Clay (D-St. Louis, Mo.)**: said the Brady Bill is "the minimum step" that Con-

---

[249] Charles Krauthammer, DISARM THE CITIZENRY. BUT NOT YET. Washington Post, Apr. 5, 1996, https://www.washingtonpost.com/archive/opinions/1996/04/05/disarm-the-citizenry-but-not-yet/8efbb5da-fd5e-48c9-8a83-0fb41c728338/?utm_term=.fc7653fc6fcc.

[250] Richard Harris, *A Reporter at Large: Handguns,* New Yorker, July 26, 1976, at 53, 58, available at http://archives.newyorker.com/?i=1976-07-26#folio=052.

gress should take to control handguns. "We need much stricter gun control, and eventually we should bar the ownership of handguns except in a few cases."[251]

- Barbara Fass (Mayor of Stockton, California):

  - Peter Jennings: "And the effect of the assault rifle ban in Stockton? The price went up, gun stores sold out and police say that fewer than 20 were turned in. Still, some people in Stockton argue you cannot measure the effect that way. They believe there's value in making a statement that the implements of violence are unacceptable in our culture."

  - Barbara Fass: "I think you have to do it a step at a time and I think that is what the NRA is most concerned about, is that it will happen one very small step at a time, so that by the time people have 'woken up' -- quote -- to what's happened, it's gone farther than what they feel the consensus of American citizens would be. But it does have to go one step at a time and the beginning of the banning of semi-assault military weapons, that are military weapons, not 'household' weapons, is the first step."[252]

---

[251] Robert L. Koenig, *NRA-Backed Measure May Derail Brady Bill*, St. Louis Post Dispatch 1A (May 8, 1991).

[252] ABC News Special, *Peter Jennings Reporting: Guns* (Apr. 11, 1991).

- **Dianne Feinstein**: "Mayor Dianne Feinstein moved yesterday to make San Francisco the nation's first major city to ban handguns for personal use."[253]

- **Sen. John H. Chafee (R.-R.I.)**: "I shortly will introduce legislation banning the sale, manufacture or possession of handguns (with exceptions for law enforcement and licensed target clubs). . . . It is time to act. We cannot go on like this. Ban them!"[254]

- **Former Secretary of Housing and Urban Development, San Antonio Mayor Henry Cisneros, Baltimore Mayor Kurt Schmoke, and 73 other signatories (mostly academics)**: signed the Communitarian Network›s *The Case for Domestic Disarmament*, which among other things said: "There is little sense in gun registration. What we need to significantly enhance public safety is domestic disarmament . . . Domestic disarmament entails the removal of arms from private hands . . . Given the proper political support by the people who oppose the pro-gun lobby, legislation to remove the guns from

---

[253] Feinstein Seeks To Ban Handguns In San Francisco, Washington Post, Feb. 26, 1982, https://www.washingtonpost.com/archive/politics/1982/02/26/feinstein-seeks-to-ban-handguns-in-san-francisco/8055b771-5caa-4bb1-908d-91ad68546c86/?noredirect=on&utm_term=.fd8a9d236c50.

[254] *In View of Handguns' Effects, There's Only One Answer: A Ban*, Minneapolis Star Tribune, June 15, 1992, at 13A.

private hands, acts like the legislation drafted by Senator John Chafee [to ban handguns], can be passed in short order."[255]

- **Rep. Bobby Rush (D-Ill.)**: "My staff and I right now are working on a comprehensive gun-control bill. We don't have all the details, but for instance, regulating the sale and purchase of bullets. Ultimately, I would like to see the manufacture and possession of handguns banned except for military and police use. But that's the endgame. And in the meantime, there are some specific things that we can do with legislation."[256]
- **Rep. Major Owens (D-Brooklyn, N.Y.)**: "Mr. Speaker, my bill prohibits the importation, exportation, manufacture, sale, purchase, transfer, receipt, possession, or transportation of handguns and handgun ammunition. It establishes a 6-month grace period for the turning in of handguns. It provides many exceptions for gun clubs, hunting clubs, gun collectors, and other people of that kind."[257]
- **LA Times Editorial**: Why should America adopt a policy of near-zero tolerance for private

---

[255] Amitai Etzioni & Steven Hellend, *The Case for Domestic Disarmament*, https://www2.gwu.edu/~ccps/pop_disarm.html.

[256] Evan Osnos, *Bobby Rush; Democrat, U.S. House of Representatives,* Chicago Tribune, Dec. 5, 1999, at C3.

[257] 139 Cong. Rec. H9088 at H9094, Nov. 10, 1993.

gun ownership? Because it's the only alternative to the present insanity. Without both strict limits on access to new weapons and aggressive efforts to reduce the supply of existing weapons, no one can be safer.[258]

- **Washington Post**: "No presidential candidate has yet come out for the most effective proposal to check the terror of gunfire: a ban on the general sale, manufacture and ownership of handguns as well as assault-style weapons."[259]
- **Michael Gartner (then-president of NBC News)**: "There is no reason for anyone in this country, anyone except a police officer or a military person, to buy, to own, to have, to use a handgun. I used to think handguns could be controlled by laws about registration, by laws requiring waiting periods for purchasers, by laws making sellers check out the past of buyers. I now think the only way to control handgun use in this country is to prohibit the guns.

---

[258] Editorial, *Taming The Monster: Get Rid of the Guns: More Firearms won't make America safer--they will only accelerate and intensify the heartache and bloodshed,* Los Angeles Times, Dec. 28, 1993, http://articles.latimes.com/1993-12-28/local/me-6058_1_gun-violence.

[259] Editorial, *Guns Along the Campaign Trail,* Washington Post, July 19, 1999, at A18, available at https://www.highbeam.com/doc/1P2-600441.html.

And the only way to do that is to change the Constitution."[260]

- **Rosie O'Donnell**: "I would like to dispute that. Truthfully. I know it's an amendment. I know it's in the Constitution. But you know what? Enough! I would like to say, I think there should be a law -- and I know this is extreme -- that no one can have a gun in the U.S. If you have a gun, you go to jail. Only the police should have guns."[261]

- **Roger Rosenblatt (Time Magazine columnist)**: "My guess [is] . . . that the great majority of Americans are saying they favor gun control when they really mean gun banishment . . . I think the country has long been ready to restrict the use of guns, except for hunting rifles and shotguns, and now I think we're prepared to get rid of the damned things entirely -- the handguns, the semis and the automatics."[262]

- **Jack E. White (*Time* correspondent)**: "Whatever is being proposed is way too namby-pamby. I mean, for example, we're talking about limiting

---

[260] Michael Gartner, *Glut of Guns: What Can We Do About Them?*, USA Today, Jan. 16, 1992, at 9A.

[261] Shannon Hawkins, *Rosie Takes on the NRA*, Ottawa Sun, April 29, 1999, at 55 (quoting talk show hostess Rosie O'Donnell).

[262] Roger Rosenblatt, *Get Rid of the Damned Things*, Time, Aug. 9, 1999, at 38, http://content.time.com/time/magazine/article/0,9171,28831,00.html.

people to one gun purchase or handgun purchase a month. Why not just ban the ownership of handguns when nobody needs one? Why not just ban semi-automatic rifles? Nobody needs one.»[263]

- **Thomas Winship (former editor of the Boston Globe)**: "Investigate the NRA with renewed vigor. It may be on the run, but its spokesman claims membership ($25 annual dues) is up 600,000 over 10 years ago. Print names of elected officials who take NRA funds. Interview them. Support all forms of gun licensing; in fact, all the causes NRA opposes."[264]
- **American Academy of Pediatrics**: "The American Academy of Pediatrics strongly supports gun-control legislation. We believe that handguns, deadly air guns and assault weapons should be banned."[265]

---

[263] L. Brent Bozell III, *Lock-and-Load Mode Against the 2nd,* Washington Times, May 8, 1999, at A12.

[264] *Step Up the War Against Guns,* Editor & Publisher Magazine, April 24, 1993, at 24.

[265] This quote was once available at American Association of Pediatrics, *Where We Stand,* available at http://www.aap.org/advocacy/wwestand.htm and *Where We Stand: Gun Safety,* healthchildren.org, https://www.healthychildren.org/English/safety-prevention/all-around/pages/Where-We-Stand-Gun-Safety.aspx. But the language has been replaced. *See* Aaron Sharockman, *Gun lobbyist says doctors play politics with gun question,* Politifact, Mar. 14, 2011, https://www.politifact.com/florida/statements/2011/mar/14/marion-

- **Josh Sugarmann (founder of the Violence Policy Center)**: "A gun-control movement worthy of the name would insist that President Clinton move beyond his proposals for controls -- such as expanding background checks at gun shows and stopping the import of high-capacity magazines -- and immediately call on Congress to pass far-reaching industry regulation like the Firearms Safety and Consumer Protection Act introduced by Senator Robert Torricelli, Democrat of New Jersey, and Representative Patrick Kennedy, Democrat of Rhode Island. Their measure would give the Treasury Department health and safety authority over the gun industry, and any rational regulator with that authority would ban handguns."[266]
- **Jeff Muchnick, Legislative Director, Coalition to Stop Gun Violence**: "We will never fully solve our nation's horrific problem of gun violence unless we ban the manufacture and sale of handguns and semiautomatic assault weapons."[267]

---

hammer/gun-lobbyist-says-doctors-play-politics-gun-questi/.

[266] Josh Sugarmann, *Dispense With the Half Steps and Ban Killing Machines*, Houston Chronicle, Nov. 5, 1999, at 45.

[267] Jeff Muchnick, *Better Yet, Ban All Handguns*, USA Today, Dec. 29, 1993, at 11A.

- **Michael K. Beard, Coalition to Stop Gun Violence**: "The best way to prevent gun violence is to ban handguns."[268]
- **Coalition to Stop Gun Violence**: "The goal of CSGV is the orderly elimination of the private sale of handguns and assault weapons in the United States."[269]

---

[268] Michael K. Beard, *Letters to the Editor,* WALL STREET JOURNAL, July 23, 1997, at A19.

[269] This language no longer appears on CSGV's website. According to Professor Volokh, on June 20, 2000, it was stated at this web address: Coalition to Stop Gun Violence, http://www.csgv.org/content/coalition/coal_intro.html (visited June 20, 2000). The website further provided that "The Coalition to Stop Gun Violence is composed of 44 civic, professional and religious organizations and 120,000 individual members that advocate for a ban on the sale and possession of handguns and assault weapons.»

CHAPTER 46

The phrase "assault weapon" is a political propaganda term intended by the Gun Lobby to frighten the public.

Myth: Assault weapons are like fully automatic machine guns.

Truth:

- Lamenting the lack of enthusiasm for a handgun ban, the founder of the Violence Policy Center, Josh Sugarmann, explained in a 1988 strategy memo that targeting "assault weapons" would "strengthen the handgun restriction lobby" because:

> The weapons' menacing looks, coupled with the public's confusion over fully automatic machine guns versus semiautomatic assault weapons—anything that looks like a machine gun is assumed to be a machine gun—can only increase

the chance of public support for
restrictions on these weapons.270

- The Stockton, California shooting occurred soon after Sugarmann issued his memo (January 17, 1989). "[T]he term 'assault weapon' was used by the media just 140 times in the two years before the mass shooting in Stockton. In the two years following the shooting, as Congress began debating what gun control advocates labeled an 'assault weapons ban,' the term was used nearly 2,600 times by the media."[271]

---

[270] *Assault Weapons and Accessories in America* 26 (Sept. 1988), available at http://www.vpc.org/studies/awaconc.htm.

[271] Aaron Blake, *Is it fair to call them 'assault weapons'?*, WASHINGTON POST, Jan. 17, 2013, https://www.washingtonpost.com/news/the-fix/wp/2013/01/17/is-it-fair-to-call-them-assault-weapons/?utm_term=.859e216a35e5.

CHAPTER 47

The gun control lobby misleads the public in stating that the social costs of firearm violence is gigantic.

Myth: The social costs of gun violence is gigantic.

Truth:

- Gun use by civilians is estimated to save the country about $3.5 billion a year due to their prevention of crimes. Hence, the cost savings stemming from the avoidance of personal losses, additional police work, and court and prison expenses greatly outweigh the cost of criminal gun violence and gun accidents.[272]
- The medical cost of gun violence is only 0.16% of America's annual health care expenditures.[273]

---

[272] Sterling Burnett, National Center for Policy Analysis, *Suing Gun Manufacturers: Hazardous to Our Health*, 1999.

[273] W Max and DP Rice, *Shooting in the Dark: Estimating the Cost of Firearm Injuries*, HEALTH AFFAIRS, 1993.

CHAPTER 48

Contrary to public belief, the "powerful gun industry" does not halt all gun control legislation.

Myth: The gun industry is extremely powerful and has vast resources to lobby against all gun control legislation.

Truth:

- The firearms industry is made up of "small, marginally profitable companies," with combined revenues of $1.5 billion to $2 billion per year, thereby making it politically ineffective.[274] Maybe the powerful "gun industry" being invoked by the gun control lobby is the 100+ million adults who lawfully own firearms and do not want their civil rights impeded.

---

[274] New York Times, Mar. 18, 2000.

- In the 2002 election cycle, the total political contributions from firearm industry members, PACs and employees was under $4.4 million, which made the industry the 64th ranked contributor. In comparison, a group like the American Federation of State, County & Municipal Employees contributed $33 million.[275]

[275] OpenSecrets.org, May 2003.

CHAPTER 49

American gun makers did not sell .50-caliber rifles to terrorists.

Myth: American gun makers sold .50-calibers to terrorists, as these are their favorite weapons.

Truth:

- This myth comes from an inaccurate study conducted by the anti-gun Violence Policy Center. Americans gun manufacturers sold the rifles in question to the United States government. Years later, the U.S. government gave the rifles to Afghan freedom fighters to defeat the former Soviet Union. So there is no direct connection between gun makers and terrorists. What's more, none of the rifles in question have been used in terrorist actions.[276]

---

[276] Dave Kopel , *Guns and (Character) Assassination,* NATIONAL REVIEW, December 21, 2001.

- .50-caliber rifles are impractical for terrorists because they are heavy (20-35 pounds), impossible to conceal (typically four feet long), expensive (from $3,000 to $10,000 each, with ammunition costing $2-$5 for each round), and usually single shot (slow to reload). Not surprisingly, 50-caliber rifles have only been used in 18 crimes in the entire history of the United States.[277]

---

[277] *Weaponry: .50 Caliber Rifle Crime,* General Accounting Office Report number OSI-99-15R, revised Oct. 21, 2001.

PART X
THE SECOND AMENDMENT

CHAPTER 50

The phrase "well-regulated" in the Second Amendment means well-disciplined.

Myth: By calling for a "well-regulated" militia, the Founders intended that the right to keep and bear arms should be heavily regulated.

Truth: Here are some examples of what the Founders really meant by "well-regulated."

- The following examples of the phrase "**well-regulated**" outside of the arms context were taken from the Oxford English Dictionary, and listed by the Constitution Society:
  - 1709: "If a liberal Education has formed in us **well-regulated** Appetites and worthy Inclinations."
  - 1714: "The practice of all **well-regulated** courts of justice in the world."
  - 1812: "The equation of time ... is the adjustment of the difference of time as shown by a **well-regulated** clock and a true sun dial."
  - 1848: "A remissness for which I am sure every well-regulated person will blame the Mayor.»

- 1862: "It appeared to her **well-regulated** mind, like a clandestine proceeding."
- 1894: "The newspaper, a never wanting adjunct to every **well-regulated** American embryo city."[278]

---

[278] Brian T. Halonen, *The meaning of the phrase "well regulated" in the 2nd Amendment*, Constitution Society, http://constitution.org/cons/wellregu.htm. Note that the above are taken from the Oxford English Dictionary and bracket in time the writing of the Second Amendment.

CHAPTER 51

The American public understood the Second Amendment as protecting an individual right before the Supreme Court said so.

Myth: The Supreme Court invented the individual right to keep and bear arms in District of Columbia v. Heller, 554 U.S. 570 (2008).

Truth:

- In 2002—before the Supreme Court definitively held that the Second Amendment protects an individual right in 2008—ABC News found that "Americans overwhelmingly agree . . . that the Second Amendment guarantees the right of citizens to own guns." "After hearing the Second Amendment verbatim, 73 percent in an ABC News poll said it guarantees the right to individual gun ownership. Twenty percent said, instead, that it only guarantees the right of states to maintain militias - the government's longstanding position until the Justice Department reversed it in a U.S. Supreme Court brief last week."[279]

---

[279] *Poll: Most Support Individual Right To Arms*, ABC NEWS, May 14, 2002, https://abcnews.go.com/Politics/story?id=120984&page=1.

CHAPTER 52

The "militia" clause within the Second Amendment does not mean that the purpose of the Second Amendment is to arm the National Guard.

Myth: The militia clause is to arm the National Guard.

Truth:

- The Latin-literate Founding Fathers knew that the word "militia" is a Latin noun, meaning "military service", not an "armed group," and that is the way they used it. The word" militia" might be more meaningfully translated as "defense service", associated with a "defense duty," which attaches to individuals as much as to groups. Put another way, we are all militias of one when we are alone. In the broadest sense, militia is the exercise of civic virtue.[280]

---

280 *Militia,* The Constitution Society.

- 'We have found no historical evidence that the Second Amendment was intended to convey militia power to the states, limit the federal government's power to maintain a standing army, or applies only to members of a select militia while on active duty. All of the evidence indicates that the Second Amendment, like other parts of the Bill of Rights, applies to and protects individual Americans."[281]

[281] *United States v. Emerson*, 270 F.3d 203 (5th Cir. 2001)[1], cert. denied, 536 U.S. 907 (2002).

PART XI
MASS SHOOTINGS

CHAPTER 53

The United States does not have the highest rate of mass shootings and mass shooting fatalities among developed countries.

Myth: Mass shootings do not happen in other countries.

Truth:

- In 2016, Adam Lankford claimed that the United States accounted for 31% of the world's public mass shooters during the 47-year period from 1966 to 2012. This claim had four years of extensive worldwide media coverage. But when Lankford finally made his datasets available to other academics in 2020, he revealed that he used a definition of public mass shootings that is inconsistent with those of the FBI, the Department of Homeland Security, and the New York Police Department that he had claimed to be following. Dr. John R. Lott and Professor Carlisle E. Moody found that Lankford's dataset does not even follow his own definition, as he has excluded foreign cases that are consistent with his definition and included cases for the United States that do not fit his definition. As a result, his handling of data greatly exaggerates the U.S. share of public mass shooters. Dr. Lott and Professor Moody used an improved dataset and estimated the number of shooters using the NYPD definition that Lankford claims to use. They found that the U.S. only has 1.25% of the world's mass shooters.[282]

- Legal scholar David Hardy points out that: "The record death toll from a mass shooting came in Norway, in 2011: 67 deaths. The record death toll from a mass killing of any type came in China, in 2001; the killer used bombs to take 108 lives. In 1982 a berserk South Korean policeman killed 56 (the same number that died in our worst shooting, in Las Vegas), in 2007 two Ukrainians killed 25 with a hammer and a pipe, in 1986 a Columbian used a six-shot revolver to kill 29 in a Bogota restaurant."[283]
- Research by Jaclyn Schildkraut and Jaymi Elsass found that "despite the United States having the greatest number of mass shooting incidents, the rate of those killed (0.15 per 100,000) is lower than in Norway (1.30), Findland (0.34), and Switzerland

---

282 John R. Lott, Jr. and Carlisle E. Moody, *Brought Into the Open: How the U.S. Compares to Other Countries in the Rate of Public Mass Shooters,* 17(1) ECON JOURNAL WATCH 28-39 (March 2020).

283 David T. Hardy, MASS KILLINGS: MYTH, REALITY, AND SOLUTIONS 4 (2018).

(0.17). The same pattern emerges when looking at the total number of victims."[284]

- John Lott's research on mass shootings from January 2009 to December 2015 found that the United States had only the 11th highest death rate from mass shootings per million people. At 0.089, the United States was well below the top country, Norway, at 1.888.[285]

- The following Gun Facts chart shows, "On a per population basis, the United States ranks fourth behind three European countries or eighth when a broader set of non-conflict countries are examined."[286]

---

[284] Jaclyn Schildkraut & Jaymi Elsass, MASS SHOOTINGS: MEDIA, MYTHS, AND REALITIES 113 (2016).

[285] John Lott, *Comparing Death Rates from Mass Public Shootings and Mass Public Violence in the US and Europe*, CRIME RESEARCH PREVENTION CENTER, https://crimeresearch.org/2015/06/comparing-death-rates-from-mass-public-shootings-in-the-us-and-europe/.

[286] *Mass Shootings: Media, Myths, and Realities*, Jaclyn Schildkraut, H. Jaymi Elsass; *The facts shoot holes in Obama's claim that US is only host to mass killings*, John Lott, December 2015.

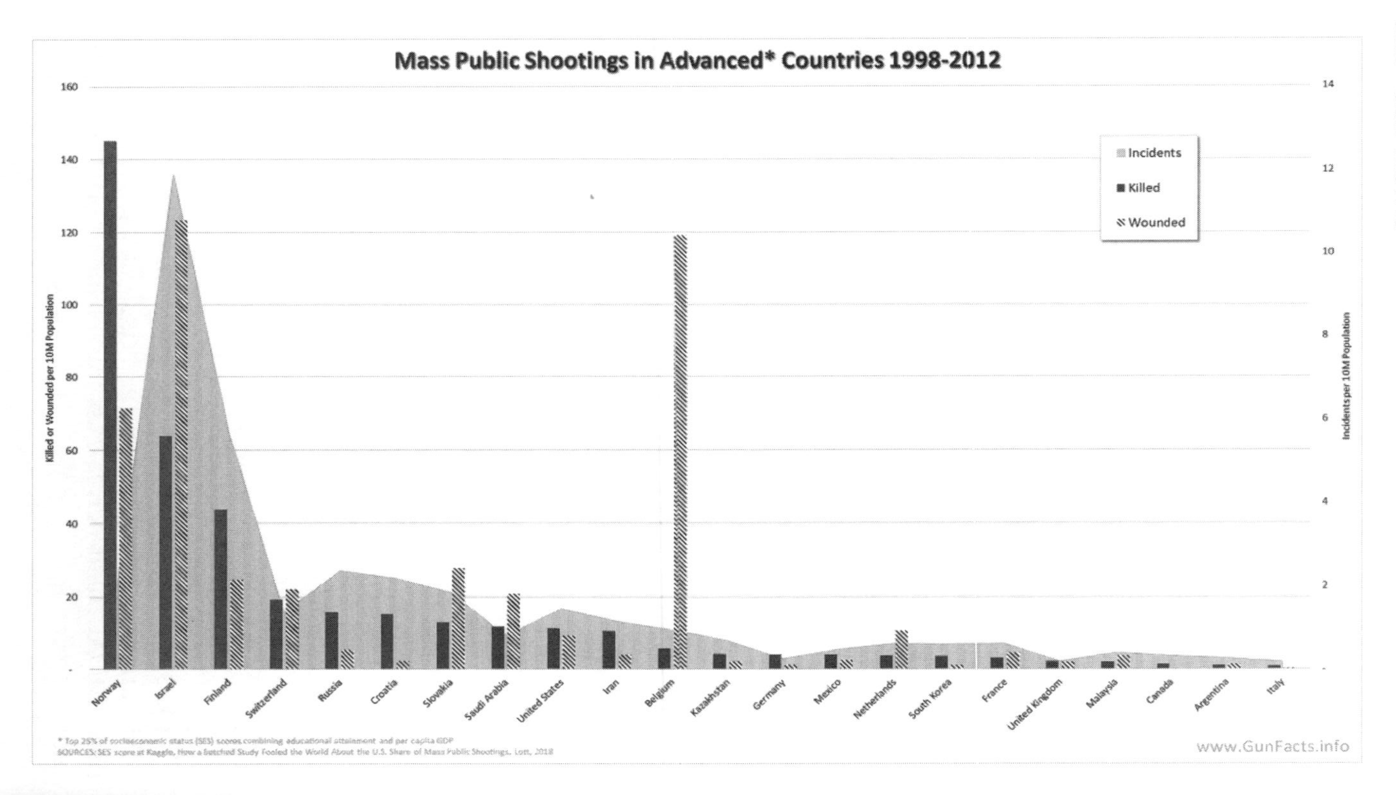
Mass Public Shootings in Advanced* Countries 1998-2012
Incidents
Killed
Wounded
Killed or Wounded per 10M Population
Incidents per 10M Population
160
140
120
100
80
60
40
20
14
12
10
8
6
4
2
Norway
Israel
Finland
Switzerland
Russia
Croatia
Slovakia
Saudi Arabia
United States
Iran
Belgium
Kazakhstan
Germany
Mexico
Netherlands
South Korea
France
United Kingdom
Malaysia
Canada
Argentina
Italy
* Top 25% of socioeconomic status (SES) scores combining educational attainment and per capita GDP
SOURCES: SES score at Kaggle, How a Botched Study Fooled the World About the U.S. Share of Mass Public Shootings, Lott, 2018
www.GunFacts.info

CHAPTER 54

Armed civilians can thwart mass shootings.

Myth: A "good guy with a gun" never stops a mass shooting.

Truth:

- One study shows that there are 1/8th the number of casualties when armed citizens responding to rampage killers, compared to when police intervene. This suggests that waiting on police to arrive can result in eight times as many deaths.[287]
- Since 2014, The Crime Prevention Research Center has been systematically collecting data to compile a list of cases in which a concealed carry permit-holder has stopped a mass shooting. The list current includes more than 40 examples.[288]
- A study of mass-shootings from 1977 to 1995 "support[s] the hypothesis that concealed handgun or shall issue laws reduce the number of mul-

[287] Davi Barker, Auditing Shooting Rampage Statistics, July 2013 and updated thereafter.

[288] *Compiling Cases where concealed handgun permit holders have stopped mass public shootings and other mass attacks*, Crime Prevention Research Center, https://crimeresearch.org/2019/05/uber-driver-in-chicago-stops-mass-public-shooting/.

tiple victim public shootings. Attackers are deterred and the number of people injured or killed per attack is also reduced."[289] "Not only does the passage of a shall issue law have a significant impact on multiple shootings but it is the only law related variable that appears to have a significant impact. Other law enforcement efforts from the arrest rate for murder to the death penalty to waiting periods and background checks are not systematically related to multiple shootings. We also find that shall issue laws deter both the number of multiple shootings and the amount of harm per shooting."[290]

---

[289] John Lott & William M. Landes, *Multiple Victim Public Shootings, Bombings, and Right-to-Carry Concealed Handgun Laws: Contrasting Private and Public Law Enforcement*, University of Chicago Law School: Chicago Unbound 20 (1999), https://citeseerx.ist.psu.edu/viewdoc/download?doi=10.1.1.825.9058&rep=rep1&type=pdf.

[290] John Lott & William M. Landes, *Multiple Victim Public Shootings, Bombings, and Right-to-Carry Concealed Handgun Laws: Contrasting Private and Public Law Enforcement*, University of Chicago Law School: Chicago Unbound 20–21 (1999), https://citeseerx.ist.psu.edu/viewdoc/download?doi=10.1.1.825.9058&rep=rep1&type=pdf.

CHAPTER 55

A nexus exists between mental illness and mass shootings.

Myth: Mass shootings are about guns, not mental illness.

Truth:

- Researchers Grant Duwe and Michael Rocque found that "at least 54% of the 185 public mass shootings that took place in the United States from 1900 through 2017 were carried out by people who had either been diagnosed with a mental disorder or demonstrated signs of serious mental illness prior to the attack."[291]

---

[291] Grant Duwe & Michael Rocque, *Actually, there is a clear link between mass shootings and mental illness*, L.A. Times, Feb. 23, 2018, https://www.latimes.com/opinion/op-ed/la-oe-duwe-rocque-mass-shootings-mental-illness-20180223-story.html.

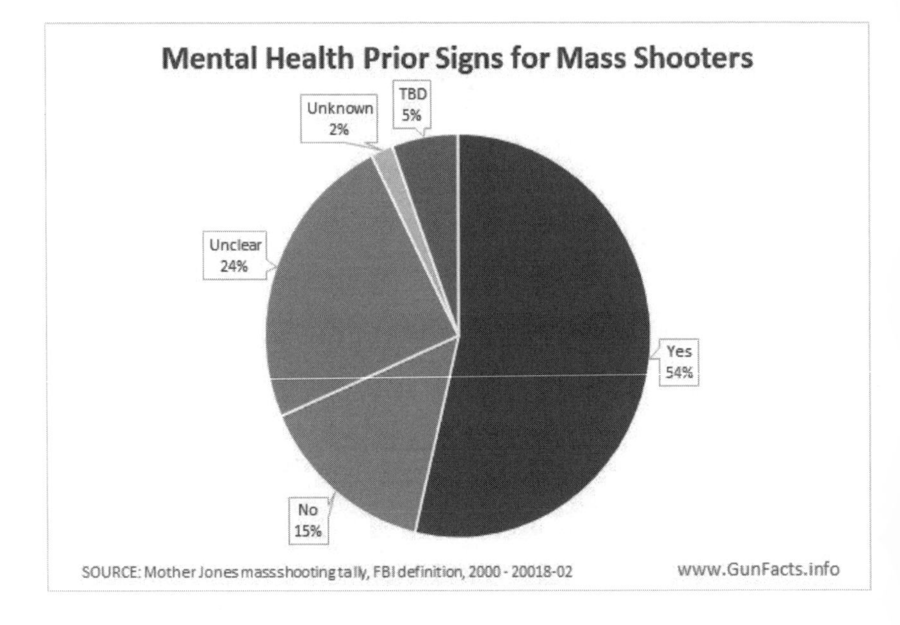

- Mother Jones found that of the 62 mass shooters it researched, "at least 38 of them displayed signs of possible mental health problems prior to the killings."[292]
- "Both rates [above] are considerably higher than those found in the general population — more than three times higher than the rate of mental illness found among American adults, and about

[292] Mark Follman, *Mass Shootings: Maybe What We Need is a Better Mental-Health Policy*, MOTHER JONES, Nov. 9, 2012, https://www.motherjones.com/politics/2012/11/jared-loughner-mass-shootings-mental-illness/.

15 times higher than the rate of serious mental illness found among American adults."[293]

- "Peer-reviewed research has shown that individuals with major mental disorders (those that substantially interfere with life activities) are more likely to commit violent acts, especially if they abuse drugs."[294]
- Duwe and Rocque explained that, "Although the link between mass shootings and mental illness has only recently gained widespread recognition, the correlation itself is longstanding. Indeed, we see it in some of the earliest such shootings in the U.S. Gilbert Twigg, who opened fire on a concert crowd in Winfield, Kan., in 1903, killing nine, had displayed signs of paranoia beforehand. Howard Unruh, who shot and killed 13 people in Camden, N.J., in 1949, was later diagnosed with paranoid

---

[293] Grant Duwe & Michael Rocque, *Actually, there is a clear link between mass shootings and mental illness*, L.A. Times, Feb. 23, 2018, https://www.latimes.com/opinion/op-ed/la-oe-duwe-rocque-mass-shootings-mental-illness-20180223-story.html.

[294] Grant Duwe & Michael Rocque, *Actually, there is a clear link between mass shootings and mental illness*, L.A. Times, Feb. 23, 2018, https://www.latimes.com/opinion/op-ed/la-oe-duwe-rocque-mass-shootings-mental-illness-20180223-story.html (citing Eric Silver, *Understanding the Relationship Between Mental Disorder and Violence: The Need for a Criminological Perspective*, Law and Human Behavior, Vol. 30(6) (Dec. 2006), available at https://psycnet.apa.org/doiLanding?doi=10.1007%2Fs10979-006-9018-z).

schizophrenia. (Both were also Army veterans who had seen combat.)"[295]

- In his book on mass shootings, David Hardy identified several mental health issues that mass killers suffered from, including narcissistic personality disorder, psychopathy, sadism, depression, and schizophrenia.[296]

---

[295] Grant Duwe & Michael Rocque, *Actually, there is a clear link between mass shootings and mental illness*, L.A. TIMES, Feb. 23, 2018, https://www.latimes.com/opinion/op-ed/la-oe-duwe-rocque-mass-shootings-mental-illness-20180223-story.html.

[296] David T. Hardy, MASS KILLINGS: MYTH, REALITY, AND SOLUTIONS 13-21 (2018).

PART XII
ACCIDENTS

CHAPTER 56

Firearm accidents are uncommon.

Myth: New gun control is needed to address the epidemic of fatal firearm accidents.[297]

Truth:

- Fatal firearm accidents are rare. While many estimates place the number of civilian owned firearms in America between 300- and 400-million,[298] there are only a few hundred accidental deaths from firearms each year. In 2016, 495 deaths were caused by an accidental discharge (up slightly from 489 in 2015). These made up 1.28 percent of the 38,658 firearm deaths that year (the large majority of which are suicides), and 0.3 percent of all 161,374 accidental deaths. By comparison, there were 58,335 accidental fatal poisonings, 40,327 deaths from motor vehicle accidents, 34,673 deaths

---

[297] "The National Rifle Association suggestion that criminals not guns kill people, ignores the fact that thousands are killed each year, many of them children, from accidental discharge of guns…" Amitai Etzioni & Steven Hellend, The Case for Domestic Disarmament, GWU.EDU, https://www2.gwu.edu/~ccps/pop_disarm.html.

[298] The Small Arms Survey recently estimated the number at 393,300,000. Aaron Karp, *Estimating Global Civilian-Held Firearms Numbers*, Small Arms Survey 4 (2018).

from accidental fallings, 3,786 accidental drownings, and 2,803 deaths from accidental exposure to smoke, fire, and flames.[299]

- The following graph presents a WISQARS computed Data Visualization of all unintentional deaths in 2016.[300]

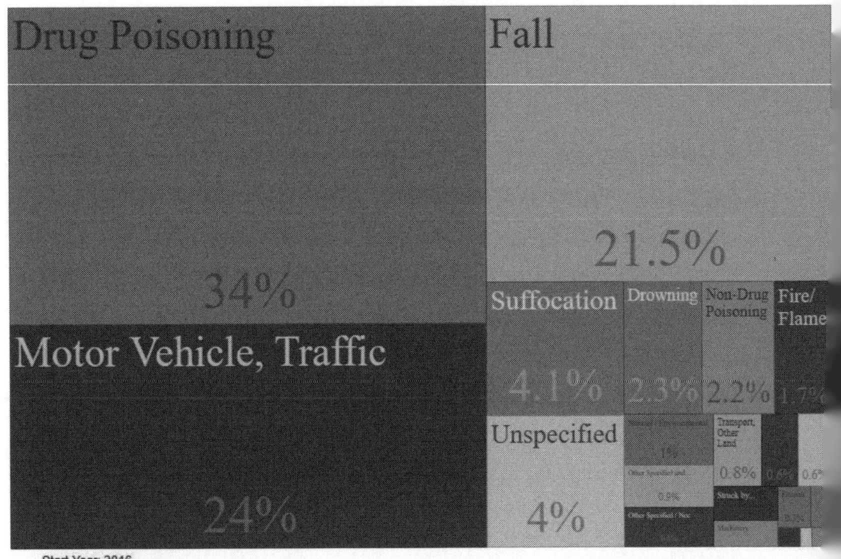

Firearms (0.3%

---

[299] Center for Disease Control and Prevention, *Fatal Injury Data*, WISQARS, available at https://webappa.cdc.gov/sasweb/ncipc/mortrate.html (run query).

[300] Center for Disease Control and Prevention, WISQARS Fatal Injury Data Visualization, available at https://wisqars-viz.cdc.gov/ (run query). Query terms are as stated in the lower left area below the graph.

- The Small Arms Survey recently estimated that there are 393,300,000 firearms in America.[301] Using this figure and the CDC's number of fatalities from accidental discharges, for every firearm that was used in an accidental fatality, 794,545 firearms were not.

- The accidental fatality rate—including among children—has been sharply decreasing for the last four decades, despite a sharp increase in the number of firearms. The following table and graph show that from 1948 to 2014, the number of firearms per capita in the United States has increased 214 percent (from 0.36 guns per person to 1.13), while the fatal gun accident rate has declined by 88 percent (from 1.55 fatal accidents per 100,000 persons to 0.18). The table also shows that from 1950 (when accident data regarding children became available) to 2014, the accidental firearm fatality rate for children (ages 0 to 14) fell by 92 percent (from 1.10 per 100,000 persons to 0.09).

- The following table from the Second Amendment textbook, *Firearms Law and the Second Amendment: Regulation, Rights and Policy*, shows the Rate of Gun Ownership vs. Rate of Gun Homicide and Fatal Gun Accidents.[302]

---

301 Aaron Karp, *Estimating Global Civilian-Held Firearms Numbers*, Small Arms Survey 4 (2018).

302 The table is from Nicholas Johnson, et al., Firearms Law and the Second Amendment: Regulation, Rights and Policy 9–12 (2d ed. 2017). Sources cited by this textbook for the table are:

Year	Population (in 1,000s)	Total gun stock	Guns per capita	Murder and nonnegligent manslaughter per 100,000 persons
1948	146,091	53,203,031	0.36	5.6
1949	148,666	55,406,460	0.37	5.1
1950	151,871	57,902,081	0.38	5.0
1951	153,970	59,988,664	0.39	4.7
1952	156,369	61,946,315	0.40	4.9
1953	158,946	63,945,235	0.40	4.6
1954	161,881	65,558,052	0.40	4.6
1955	165,058	67,387,135	0.41	4.3
1956	168,078	69,435,933	0.41	4.4
1957	171,178	71,416,509	0.42	4.3
1958	174,153	73,163,450	0.42	4.3
1959	177,136	75,338,188	0.43	4.5
1960	179,972	77,501,065	0.43	5.1
1961	182,976	79,536,616	0.43	4.8
1962	185,739	81,602,984	0.44	4.6
1963	188,434	83,834,808	0.44	4.6
1964	191,085	86,357,701	0.45	4.9
1965	193,457	89,478,922	0.46	5.1
1966	195,499	93,000,989	0.48	5.6
1967	197,375	97,087,751	0.49	6.2
1968	199,312	102,302,251	0.51	6.9
1969	201,298	107,111,820	0.53	7.3
1970	203,798.7	111,917,733	0.55	7.9
1971	206,817.5	116,928,781	0.57	8.6
1972	209,274.9	122,304,980	0.58	9.0
1973	211,349.2	128,016,673	0.61	9.4

Fatal gun accidents	FGAs for ages 0-14	Population age 0 to 14 (in 1,000s)	Fatal gun accidents per 100,000 persons	FGAs per 100,000 persons for ages 0-14
2,270			1.55	
2,326			1.56	
2,174	451	40,853	1.43	1.10
2,247	520	42,065	1.46	1.24
2,210	519	43,377	1.41	1.20
2,277	498	44,759	1.43	1.11
2,281	527	46,266	1.41	1.14
2,120	522	47,867	1.28	1.09
2,202	508	49,449	1.31	1.03
2,369	549	51,080	1.38	1.07
2,172	538	52,699	1.25	1.02
2,258	542	54,345	1.27	1.00
2,334	544	55,971	1.30	0.97
2,204	507	56,046	1.20	0.90
2,092	456	56,019	1.13	0.81
2,263	538	55,946	1.20	0.96
2,275	500	55,835	1.19	0.90
2,344	494	55,619	1.21	0.89
2,558	535	55,287	1.31	0.97
2,896	598	54,890	1.47	1.09
2,394	527	54,492	1.20	0.97
2,309	455	54,089	1.15	0.84
2,406	506	53,803	1.18	0.94
2,360	481	53,835	1.14	0.89
2,442	554	53,700	1.17	1.03
2,618	541	53,450	1.24	1.01

(continued)

Year	Population (in 1,000s)	Total gun stock	Guns per capita	Murder and nonnegligent manslaughter per 100,000 persons
1974	213,333.6	134,587,281	0.63	9.8
1975	215,456.6	139,915,125	0.65	9.6
1976	217,553.9	145,650,789	0.67	8.8
1977	219,760.9	150,748,000	0.69	8.8
1978	222,098.2	156,164,518	0.70	9.0
1979	224,568.6	161,888,861	0.72	9.7
1980	227,224.7	167,681,587	0.74	10.2
1981	229,465.7	173,262,755	0.76	9.8
1982	231,664.4	178,218,890	0.77	9.1
1983	233,792.0	182,273,263	0.78	8.3
1984	235,824.9	186,683,867	0.79	7.9
1985	237,923.7	190,658,136	0.80	8.0
1986	240,132.8	194,182,072	0.81	8.6
1987	242,288.9	198,526,508	0.82	8.3
1988	244,499.0	203,306,821	0.83	8.5
1989	246,819.2	208,489,609	0.84	8.7
1990	249,438.7	212,823,547	0.85	9.4
1991	252,127.4	216,695,946	0.86	9.8
1992	254,994.5	222,067,343	0.87	9.3
1993	257,746.1	228,660,966	0.89	9.5
1994	260,289.2	235,604,001	0.91	9.0
1995	262,764.9	240,599,526	0.92	8.2
1996	265,189.8	245,003,546	0.92	7.4
1997	267,743.6	249,261,384	0.93	6.8
1998	270,248.0	253,771,440	0.94	6.3
1999	272,690.8	258,490,668	0.95	5.7

Fatal gun accidents	FGAs for ages 0-14	Population age 0 to 14 (in 1,000s)	Fatal gun accidents per 100,000 persons	FGAs per 100,000 persons for ages 0-14
2,513	532	53,163	1.18	1.00
2,380	495	52,895	1.10	0.94
2,059	428	52,605	0.95	0.81
1,982	392	52,325	0.90	0.75
1,806	349	52,060	0.81	0.67
2,004	372	51,523	0.89	0.72
1,955	316	51,369	0.86	0.62
1,871	298	51,275	0.82	0.58
1,756	279	51,367	0.76	0.54
1,695	243	51,458	0.73	0.47
1,668	287	51,580	0.71	0.56
1,649	278	51,616	0.69	0.54
1,452	234	51,592	0.60	0.45
1,440	247	51,965	0.59	0.48
1,501	277	52,604	0.61	0.53
1,489	273	53,405	0.60	0.51
1,416	236	54,065	0.57	0.44
1,441	227	55,352	0.57	0.41
1,409	216	56,297	0.55	0.38
1,521	205	57,203	0.59	0.36
1,356	185	57,918	0.52	0.32
1,225	181	58,380	0.47	0.31
1,134	138	58,850	0.43	0.23
981	142	59,217	0.37	0.24
866	121	59,659	0.32	0.20
824	88	59,955	0.30	0.15

(continued)

Year	Population (in 1,000s)	Total gun stock	Guns per capita	Murder and nonnegligent manslaughter per 100,000 persons
2000	281,421.9	263,208,364	0.94	5.5
2001	285,317.6	267,335,304	0.94	5.6
2002	287,973.9	272,180,680	0.95	5.6
2003	290,809.8	276,813,674	0.95	5.7
2004	293,655.4	281,683,638	0.96	5.5
2005	296,507.1	286,837,125	0.97	5.6
2006	299,398.5	292,555,450	0.98	5.8
2007	301,621.2	299,017,274	0.99	5.7
2008	304,059.7	305,894,116	1.01	5.4
2009	307,006.6	314,862,296	1.03	5.0
2010	308,745.5	322,863,994	1.05	4.8
2011	311,721.6	332,223,910	1.07	4.7
2012	314,112.0	340,802,520	1.08	4.7
2013	316,497.5	351,647,312	1.11	4.5
2014	318,857.0	360,697,938	1.13	4.5

Fatal gun accidents	FGAs for ages 0-14	Population age 0 to 14 (in 1,000s)	Fatal gun accidents per 100,000 persons	FGAs per 100,000 persons for ages 0-14
776	86	60,253	0.28	0.14
802	72	60,435	0.28	0.12
762	60	60,646	0.26	0.10
730	56	60,738	0.25	0.09
649	63	60,822	0.22	0.10
789	75	60,953	0.27	0.12
642	54	61,023	0.21	0.08
613	65	61,295	0.20	0.11
592	62	61,570	0.19	0.10
554	48	61,883	0.18	0.08
606	55	61,227	0.20	0.09
591	69	61,176	0.19	0.12
548	58	61,124	0.17	0.11
505	69	61,086	0.16	0.14
586	50	61,079	0.18	0.09

- The following graph, also from the Second Amendment textbook, *Firearms Law and the Second Amendment: Regulation, Rights and Policy*, shows the fatal gun accident rate versus the number of guns per capita from 1948-2014.[303]

Fatal gun accidents from Centers for Disease Control, *Compressed Mortality File, available at* http://wonder.cdc.gov/mortSQL.html (run query) and Gary Kleck, Targeting Guns, *supra*, at 323-24. The gun supply figures through 1994 are from Kleck, TARGETING GUNS, *supra*, at 96-97 (providing citations for all the data). Additions to the gun supply from 1995 through 2014 are from the 2014 edition of ATF's Commerce in Firearms in the United States ex. 1-3, *available at* https://www.atf.gov/resource-center/docs/firearmscommerceannualstatisticalreport2014pdf/download, plus the 2014 ATF Annual Firearms Manufacture and Export Report, *available at* https://www.atf.gov/firearms/docs/afmer-2014-final-report-cover-revised-format-2-17-16/download. The 2005-14 figures on homicide rates are from FBI, Uniform Crime Reports, tbl.1, *available at* https://ucr.fbi.gov/crime-in-the-u.s/2014/crime-in-the-u.s.-2014/tables/table-1; Sourcebook of Criminal Justice Statistics, Estimated number and rate (per 100,000 inhabitants) of offenses known to police, by offense, United States 1960-2012, *available at* http://www.albany.edu/sourcebook/pdf/t31062012.pdf. Population age 0-14 for 2005-09 and 2010-14 from Census Bureau, Annual Estimates of the Resident Population by Sex and Five-Year Age Groups, 2010 and 2015 versions. Homicides for 1948-59, FBI Data compilation.

[303] The graph is from Nicholas Johnson, et al., FIREARMS LAW AND THE SECOND AMENDMENT: REGULATION, RIGHTS AND POLICY 24 (2d ed. 2017). The graph is based on the data in the previous table.

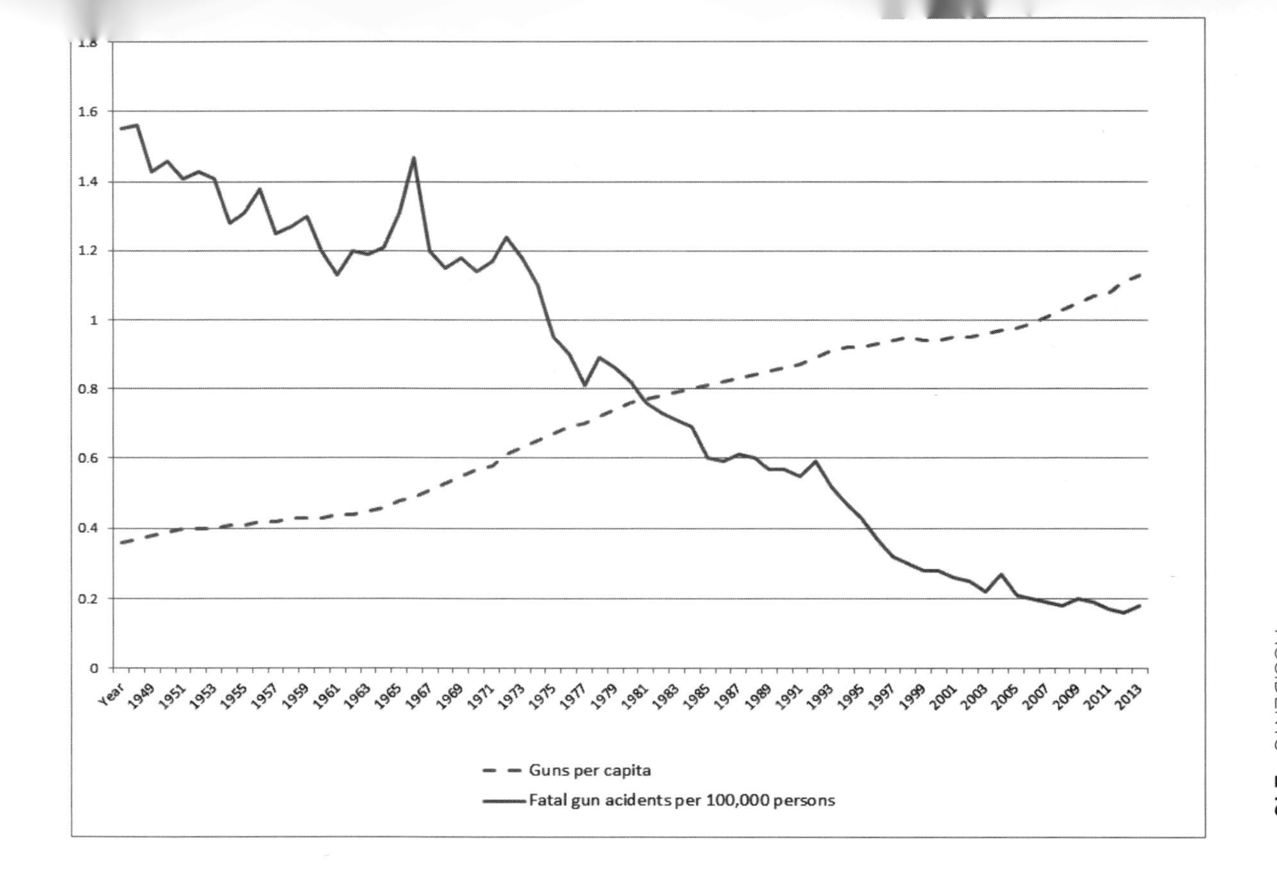

1.6
1.4
1.2
1
0.8
0.6
0.4
0.2
0
Year
1949
1951
1953
1955
1957
1959
1961
1963
1965
1967
1969
1971
1973
1975
1977
1979
1981
1983
1985
1987
1989
1991
1993
1995
1997
1999
2001
2003
2005
2007
2009
2011
2013
Guns per capita
Fatal gun acidents per 100,000 persons

- "The annual risk level for a fatal gun accident is around 0.18 per 100,000 [in the] population—less than the risk of death from taking two airplane trips a year, or getting a whooping cough vaccination."[304]
- Studies show that people who cause gun accidents tend to be more reckless in general, having high rates of "arrests, violence, alcohol abuse, highway crashes, and citations for moving traffic violations."[305]

---

[304] Nicholas Johnson, et al., FIREARMS LAW AND THE SECOND AMENDMENT: REGULATION, RIGHTS AND POLICY 23 (2d ed. 2017) (citing Stephen Breyer, BREAKING THE VICIOUS CIRCLE: TOWARD EFFECTIVE RISK REGULATION 5, 7 (1992) (airplane and vaccine data)).

[305] Julian Waller & Elbert Whorton, *Unintentional Shootings, Highway Crashes, and Acts of Violence*, 5 ACCIDENT ANALYSIS & PREVENTION 351, 353 (1973). *See also* Gary Kleck, TARGETING GUNS: FIREARMS AND THEIR CONTROL 307, 312 (1997).

CHAPTER 57

Citizens are sufficiently competent to use guns for protection.

Myth: Citizens are too incompetent to properly use guns of their own.

Truth:

- The odds of a defensive gun user killing an innocent person are less than 1 in 26,000, despite the fact that Americans use guns to prevent crimes around 2.5 million times a year.[306]
- As a point of comparison, about 11% of police shootings kill an innocent person.

---

[306] C. Cramer and D. Kopel, *Shall Issue: The New Wave of Concealed Handgun Permit Laws*, Independence Institute Issue Paper, October 17, 1994.

CHAPTER 58

Handguns are *not* more likely to kill a family member than a criminal.

Myth: Handguns are 43 times more likely to kill a family member than a criminal.

Truth:

- This myth comes from a flawed study. Of the familial deaths reported in this study, 86% were suicides, and other deaths involved criminal activity between the family members, such as botched drug deals. Of the remaining deaths, the deceased family members include drug dealers, felons, violent spouses committing assault, and other criminals.[307]

[307] *See* Arthur R. Kellerman, et al. *Protection or Peril? An Analysis of Firearm-Related Deaths in the Home,* 314 New England Journal of Medicine 1557-60, June 12, 1986.

PART XIII

CONCEALED CARRY

CHAPTER 59

Allowing law-abiding citizens to concealed carry does not increase crime.

Myth: Concealed carry increases crime.

Truth:

- Results of a study of data covering the period 1980 to 2009 "suggest that restrictive concealed weapons laws may cause an increase in gun-related murders." Specifically, "states with more restrictive CCW laws had gun-related murder rates that were 10% higher."[308]
- Generally, states that do not allow concealed carry have a violent crime rate that is 11% higher than the national average.[309]

---

[308] Mark Gius, *An examination of the effects of concealed weapons laws and assault weapons bans on state-level murder rates*, APPLIED ECONOMICS LETTERS, Vol 21, No. 4, pg. 265, 267 (2014), https://www.academia.edu/28817058/An_examination_of_the_effects_of_concealed_weapons_laws_and_assault_weapons_bans_on_state-level_murder_rates.

[309] *See* FBI, Uniform Crime Reports. 2004.

- Greater rates of concealed carry permit holders tend to decrease violent crime rates even more than the "right to carry" in America. This is because studies involving "right to carry" states often include "open carry" states, which sometimes have not been shown to correlate with citizens actually carrying or owning guns.[310]

- Between 2007 and 2015, as concealed carry permits rose by 190 percent, violent crime rates dropped 18 percent and murder crime rates dropped 16 percent.[311]

- A study of concealed carry permitholders found that they are more law-abiding than law enforcement: "Concealed carry permit holders are even more law-abiding than police. Between October 1, 1987 and June 30, 2015, Florida revoked 9,999 concealed handgun permits for misdemeanors or felonies. This is an annual revocation rate of 12.8 permits per 100,000. In 2013 (the last year for which data is available), 158 permit holders were convicted of a felony or misdemeanor – a conviction rate of 22.3 per 100,000. Combining the data for Florida and Texas data, we find that permit holders are convicted of misdemeanors and felonies at less than a sixth the rate for police officers.

[310] The Heritage Foundation, *Here Are 8 Stubborn Facts on Gun Violence in America* (2018).

[311] The Heritage Foundation, *Here Are 8 Stubborn Facts on Gun Violence in America* (2018).

Among police, firearms violations occur at a rate of 16.5 per 100,000 officers. Among permit holders in Florida and Texas, the rate is only 2.4 per 100,000.10 That is just 1/7th of the rate for police officers. But there's no need to focus on Texas and Florida — the data are similar in other states."[312]

- David Kopel and Clayton Cramer wrote an article on concealed carry in 1995, when the present-day wave of concealed carry reform had recently begun. Discussing Florida's law, which began the new wave of carry laws, they found that "a murder rate that was 36% above the national average when carry reform went into effect in 1987, fell by 1991 to 4% below the national average."[313]

- Attorneys Joseph Greenlee and Jonathan Goldstein wrote an article analyzing Pennsylvania's "stand your ground" law. In the section on concealed carry permitholders, they noted:

---

[312] *Concealed Carry Permit Holders Across the United States: 2016*, Report from the Crime Prevention Research Center, 15 (2016), available at https://poseidon01.ssrn.com/delivery.php?ID=312025116122115112101124000071127120117035019009034090074026116081067085117098064101096034023121015125114119029099078068067089059082053065068068072007004114072006083084125027113003075014003105018090027002030074076096113092107105007088022104098101&EXT=pdf.

[313] Clayton E. Cramer & David B. Kopel, *Shall Issue: The New Wave of Concealed Handgun Permit Laws*, Tennessee Law Review 62:3 (Spring, 1995) 679-757. Available at http://www.davekopel.com/2A/LawRev/ShallIssue.htm.

In addition to being concerned about "gang-killers" and "road rage killers," critics expected that concealed carry permitholders would be responsible for a considerable increase in shootings. The substantial post-enactment decreases in homicides, murders, and violent crime, as well as the slight decrease in justified homicides, is therefore even more remarkable given the tremendous increase in the number of concealed carry permits that were issued after the law's enactment. In 2011 (167,656), 2012 (245,444), 2013 (269,273), 2014 (219,782), 2015 (237,344), and 2016 (300,565), sheriffs' offices throughout Pennsylvania issued a total of 1,440,064 licenses to carry firearms. Clearly, these nearly one-and-a-half-million permitholders did not endanger their communities like critics feared they would; they did not adopt a "'shoot first, ask questions later' mentality."

Residents of Potter County demonstrate just how law-abiding concealed carry permitholders can be. More than half of all adults in Potter County are licensed to carry, yet there was not a single homicide in the county in all of 2016. Indeed, there have only been three homicides classified as murder or nonnegligent manslaughter in Potter County in the 6 years since the law was passed.[314]

- An editorial writer for the San Antonio Express-News, using data from the Texas Department of Public Safety and the U.S. Census Bureau, found that "the data show that average annual arrests for all crimes among all adult males in Texas (9,508 per 100,000) is 14 times greater than the rate for concealed handgun license holders (671 per 100,000)." And, "[t]he violent crime arrest rate of all adult men in Texas (306 per 100,000) is five times greater than the violent crime arrest rate of concealed handgun license holders (62)."[315]

---

[314] Jonathan S. Goldstein & Joseph G.S. Greenlee, *Pennsylvania's Expanded Castle Doctrine: An Annotated Tour of the First Five Years*, 88 Pa. B.A. Q. 170, 180–81 (2017), available at https://docs.wixstatic.com/ugd/a979cf_2ba8ed4013bd40a8bd2a68e6501a9c35.pdf.

[315] Carl M. Hubbard, *Licensed Gun Owners are Model Texans*, San Antonio Express-News, Sep. 27, 2000, available in archives at http://nl.newsbank.com/nl-search/we/Archives?p_product=SAEC&p_theme=saec&p_action=search&p_maxdocs=200&s_dispstring=concealed%20carry%20AND%20date(6/1/2000%20to%2012/1/2000)&p_field_date-0=YMD_date&p_params_date-0=date:B,E&p_text_date-0=6/1/2000%20to%2012/1/2000)&p_field_advanced-0=&p_text_advanced-0=(concealed%20carry)&xcal_numdocs=50&p_perpage=25&p_sort=YMD_date:D&xcal_useweights=no. Dr. Hubbard added that "Since 80.5 percent of concealed handgun license holders in Texas are men, these comparisons are valid." *Id.*

- Acknowledging that fears (including his own) over concealed carry were dramatically overblown, the Harris County District Attorney said, "I'm detecting that I'm eating a lot of crow on this issue ... I think that says something, that we've gotten to this point in the year and in the third largest city in America there has not been a single charge against anyone that had anything to do with a concealed handgun."[316]
- Similarly, the president of the Dallas Police Association, Glenn White, said: "I lobbied against the law in 1993 and 1995 because I thought it would lead to wholesale armed conflict. That hasn't happened. All the horror stories I thought would come to pass didn't happen. No bogeyman. I think it's worked out well, and that says good things about the citizens who have permits. I'm a convert."[317]
- There are just over 14,500,000 people with concealed carry licenses as of 2017, and only 0.003% of them have ever killed anyone, including those that killed in self-defense.[318]

---

316 John Holmes, *In Session: Handgun Law's First Year Belies Fears of 'Blood in the Streets,"* Texas Lawyer, Dec. 9, 1996.

317 Glenn White, President of the Dallas Police Association, DALLAS MORNING NEWS, December 23, 1997.

318 See State-by-state tally from licensing records conducted by Crime Prevention Research Center.

- The Texas State Rifle Association found that from 1996 to 1998, Texas CCW holders were roughly 7.6 times less likely to be arrested for a violent crime than the general population. Based on these findings, Gun Facts created the following chart:[319]

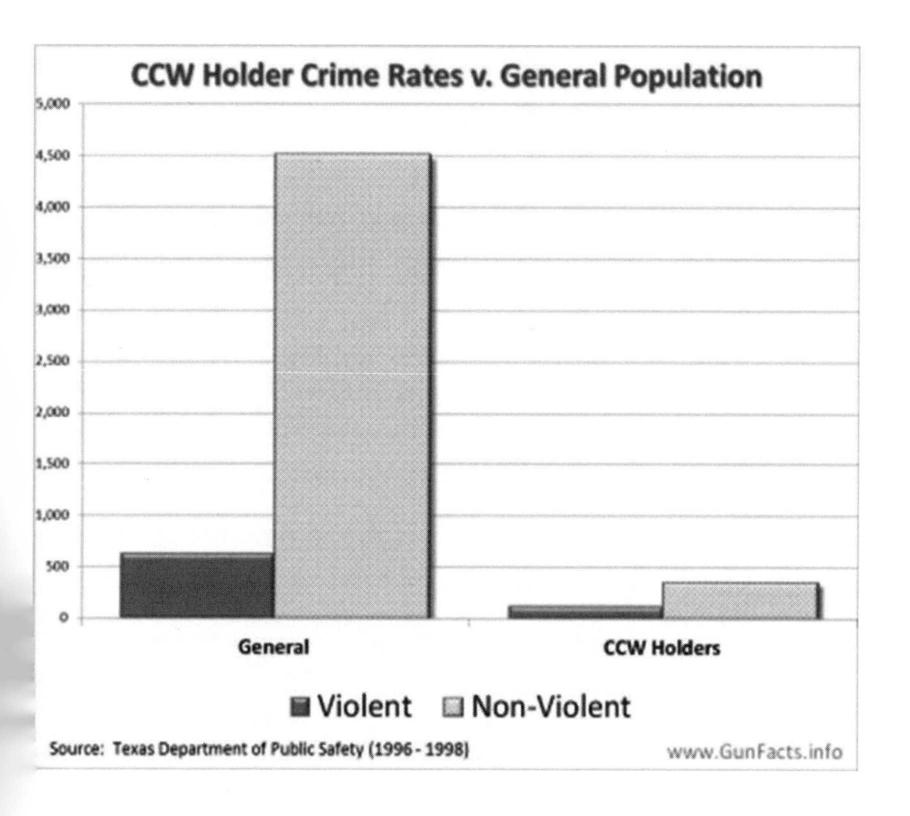

319 *Concealed Carry*, Gun Facts, http://www.gunfacts.info/gun-control-myths/concealed-carry/.

- A study by William E. Sturdevant comparing Texas concealed handgun license holders with the general population of Texas found that:[320]

Violent Crime

  - "Arrest data for Texas CHL holders indicate that violent crime is not a consequence of handgun ownership or possession."
  - "The total population of Texas has an arrest rate for violent crime that is 5.3 times higher than Texas CHL holders, based upon data from 1996 - 1999."
  - "The population of Texas that are 21 years old or older has an arrest rate for violent crime that is 5.6 times higher than Texas CHL holders, based upon data from 1996 - 1999."
  - "The population of Texas that are males 21 years old or older has an arrest rate for violent crime that is 7.9 times higher than male Texas CHL holders, based upon data from 1996 - 1999."
  - "The population of Texas that are females 21 years old or older has an arrest rate for violent crime that is 7.5 times higher than female Texas

---

[320] William E. Sturdevant, *An Analysis of the Arrest Rate of Texas Concealed Handgun License Holders as Compared to the Arrest Rate of the Entire Texas Population*, (revised version, Sept. 1, 2000), available at https://concealedguns.procon.org/sourcefiles/arrest-rate-texas.pdf.

CHL holders, based upon data from 1996 - 1999."

Murder and Non-Negligent Manslaughter

- "Arrest data for Texas CHL holders indicate that murder and non-negligent manslaughter is not a consequence of handgun ownership or possession."
- "The total population of Texas has an arrest rate for murder and non-negligent manslaughter that is 1.3 times higher than Texas CHL holders, based upon data from 1996 - 1999."
- "The population of Texas that are 21 years old or older has an arrest rate for murder and non-negligent manslaughter that is 1.3 times higher than Texas CHL holders, based upon data from 1996 - 1999."
- "The population of Texas that are males 21 years old or older has an arrest rate for murder and non-negligent manslaughter that is 1.9 times higher than male Texas CHL holders, based upon data from 1996 - 1999."
- "The population of Texas that are females 21 years old or older has an arrest rate for murder and non-negligent manslaughter that is 1.7 times higher than female Texas CHL holders, based upon data from 1996 - 1999."

Forcible Rape

- "Arrest data for Texas CHL holders indicate that forcible rape is not a consequence of handgun ownership or possession."
- "The total population of Texas has an arrest rate for forcible rape that is 42 times higher than Texas CHL holders, based upon data from 1996 - 1999."
- "The population of Texas that are 21 years old or older has an arrest rate for forcible rape that is 42 times higher than Texas CHL holders, based upon data from 1996 - 1999."
- "The population of Texas that are males 21 years old or older has an arrest rate for forcible rape that is 68 times higher than male Texas CHL holders, based upon data from 1996 - 1999."
- "No female CHL holder has been arrested for forcible rape, based upon data from 1996 - 1999."

Robbery

- "Arrest data for Texas CHL holders indicate that robbery is not a consequence of handgun ownership or possession."
- "The total population of Texas has an arrest rate for robbery that is 48 times higher than Texas CHL holders, based upon data from 1996 - 1999."

- "The population of Texas that are 21 years old or older has an arrest rate for robbery that is 35 times higher than Texas CHL holders, based upon data from 1996 - 1999."
- "The population of Texas that are males 21 years old or older has an arrest rate for robbery that is 49 times higher than male Texas CHL holders, based upon data from 1996 - 1999."
- "No female CHL holder has been arrested for robbery, based upon data from 1996 – 1999."

Aggravated Assault

- "Arrest data for Texas CHL holders indicate that aggravated assault is not a consequence of handgun ownership or possession."
- "The total population of Texas has an arrest rate for aggravated assault that is 2.2 times higher than Texas CHL holders, based upon data from 1996 - 1999."
- "The population of Texas that are 21 years old or older has an arrest rate for aggravated assault that is 2.3 times higher than Texas CHL holders, based upon data from 1996 - 1999."
- "The population of Texas that are males 21 years old or older has an arrest rate for aggravated assault that is 3.2 times higher than male Texas CHL holders, based upon data from 1996 - 1999."

- "The population of Texas that are females 21 years old or older has an arrest rate for aggravated assault that is 2.2 times higher than female Texas CHL holders, based upon data from 1996 – 1999."

Other Assault

- "Arrest data for Texas CHL holders indicate that other assault is not a consequence of handgun ownership or possession."
- "The total population of Texas has an arrest rate for other assault that is 7.6 times higher than Texas CHL holders, based upon data from 1996 - 1999."
- "The population of Texas that are 21 years old or older has an arrest rate for other assault that is 8.1 times higher than Texas CHL holders, based upon data from 1996 - 1999."
- "The population of Texas that are males 21 years old or older has an arrest rate for other assault that is 11 times higher than male Texas CHL holders, based upon data from 1996 - 1999."
- "The population of Texas that are females 21 years old or older has an arrest rate for other assault that is 20 times higher than female Texas CHL holders, based upon data from 1996 - 1999."

Family Violence

- "Less than two percent (1.9%) of the arrests of CHL holders for violent crimes that possibly involve weapons (murder, manslaughter, rape, robbery, aggravated assault) were classified as "family violence" crimes."

Non-Violent Crime

- "Arrest data for Texas CHL holders indicate that non-violent crime is not a consequence of handgun ownership or possession."
- "The total population of Texas has an arrest rate for non-violent crime that is 14 times higher than Texas CHL holders, based upon data from 1996 - 1999."
- "The population of Texas that are 21 years old or older has an arrest rate for non-violent crime that is 15 times higher than Texas CHL holders, based upon data from 1996 - 1999."
- "The population of Texas that are males 21 years old or older has an arrest rate for non-violent crime that is 20 times higher than male Texas CHL holders, based upon data from 1996 - 1999."
- "The population of Texas that are females 21 years old or older has an arrest rate for nonviolent crime that is 16 times higher than female Texas CHL holders, based upon data from 1996 - 1999."

- A 1998 report by the Florida Game and Fresh Water Fish Commission found that Floridians were twice as likely to be attacked by an alligator than by a concealed carry permitholder.[321]
- A law allowing Virginia concealed carry permitholders to carry in bars and restaurants was enacted in 2010. The Richmond Times-Dispatch analyzed its impact:

> "The number of major crimes involving firearms at bars and restaurants statewide declined 5.2 percent from July 1, 2010, to June 30, 2011, compared with the fiscal year before the law went into effect, according to crime data compiled by Virginia State Police at the newspaper's request.
>
> And overall, the crimes that occurred during the law's first year were relatively minor, and few of the incidents appeared to involve gun owners with concealed-carry permits, the analysis found.
>
> A total of 145 reported crimes with guns occurred in Virginia bars and restaurants in fiscal 2010-11, or eight fewer than the 153 incidents in fiscal 2009-10.
>
> . . .

---

[321] *Concealed Weapons/Firearms License Statistical Report*, Florida Department of State, 1998 – Florida Game and Fresh Water Fish Commission, December 1998.

> Only two fatal shootings occurred during the last fiscal year — one outside a Petersburg nightclub and the other at a Radford restaurant — but neither involved concealed-gun permit holders. And only two of the 18 aggravated assaults reported could be linked definitively to concealed-carry holders."[322]

- Gun Facts created the following chart, which illustrates how law-abiding concealed carry permit-holders were in Florida, Virginia, Arizona, and North Carolina and how the crime rate decreased in each state after laws allowing concealed carry were passed:[323]

---

322 Mark Bowes, *Gun crimes drop at Virginia bars and restaurants*, RICHMOND TIMES-DISPATCH, Aug. 14, 2011, https://www.richmond.com/archive/gun-crimes-drop-at-virginia-bars-and-restaurants/article_07eae8c7-9e74-56d6-8928-a9fe2add8ebf.html.

323 *Concealed Carry*, GUN FACTS, http://www.gunfacts.info/gun-control-myths/concealed-carry/.

State	Licenses issued	Revoked licenses	% Revoked	Violent Crime Rate Change
Florida	1,327,321	4,129	0.3%	-30.5%
Virginia	50,000	0	0.0%	-21.9%
Arizona	63,000	50	0.9%	-28.7%
North Carolina	59,597	1,274	1.2%	-26.4%
Minnesota	46,636_	12	0.03%	8.0%
Michigan	155,000	2,178	0.1%	1.4%

- Gun Facts also created this next chart, which shows how the crime rate responded to the increase in the percentage of the American population that lived in jurisdictions permitting concealed carry from 1986 to 2012.[324]

[324] *Concealed Carry*, Gun Facts, http://www.gunfacts.info/gun-control-myths/concealed-carry/.

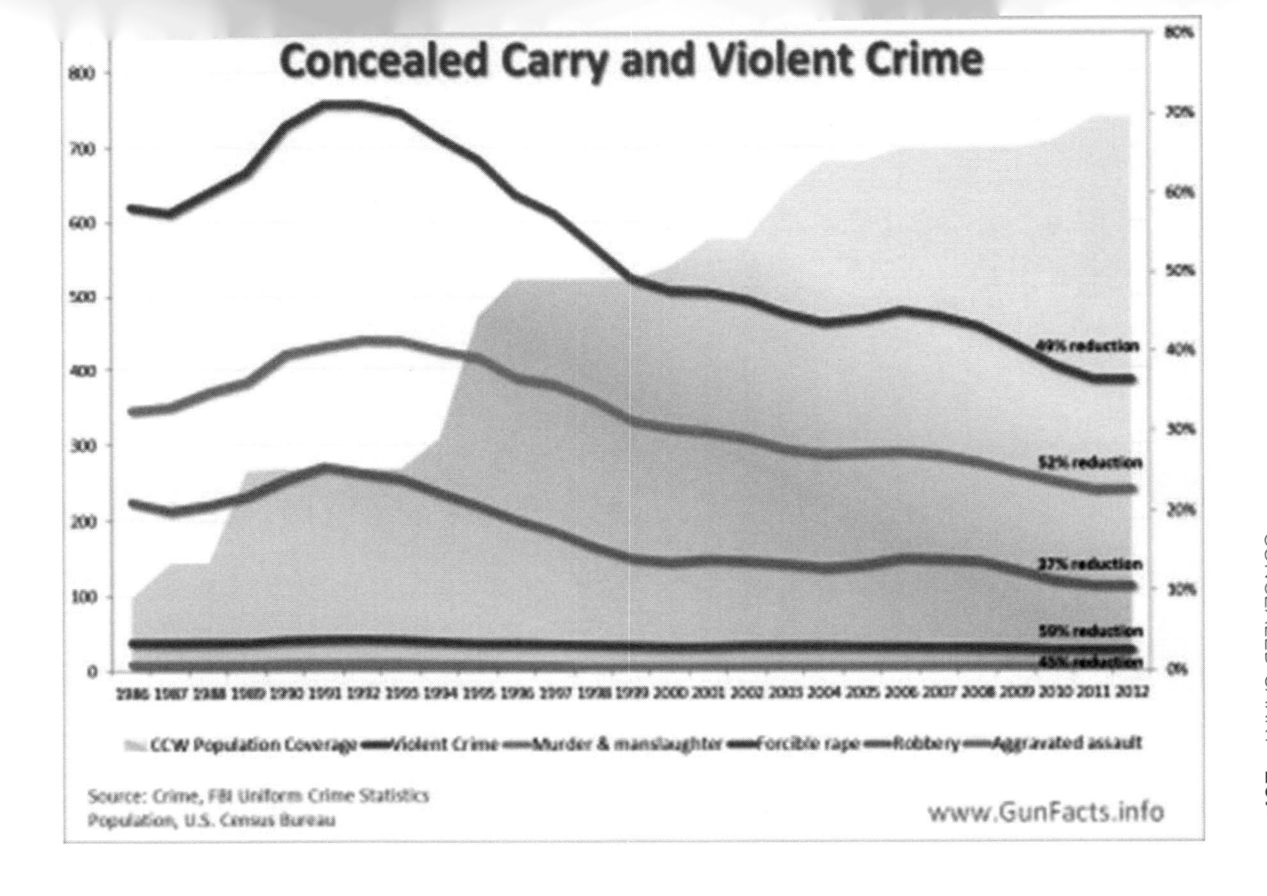

Concealed Carry and Violent Crime
800
700
600
500
400
300
200
100
0
80%
70%
60%
50%
40%
30%
20%
10%
0%
49% reduction
52% reduction
37% reduction
59% reduction
45% reduction
1986 1987 1988 1989 1990 1991 1992 1993 1994 1995 1996 1997 1998 1999 2000 2001 2002 2003 2004 2005 2006 2007 2008 2009 2010 2011 2012
CCW Population Coverage
Violent Crime
Murder & manslaughter
Forcible rape
Robbery
Aggravated assault
Source: Crime, FBI Uniform Crime Statistics
Population, U.S. Census Bureau
www.GunFacts.info

CHAPTER 60

Law enforcement largely supports concealed carry.

Myth: Law enforcement staunchly opposes concealed carry.

Truth:

- In a survey of 15,000 officers, 91% said concealed carry by civilians should be permitted "without question and without further restrictions."[325]
- 66% of police chiefs believe that citizens carrying concealed firearms reduce rates of violent crime.[326]
- In a recent survey, police officers believe that concealed carry by civilians is the most effective method to prevent mass public shootings.[327]
- Many law enforcement officers who opposed concealed carry admit that their concerns were misguided:

---

[325] *Gun Policy & Law Enforcement*, PoliceOne, March 2013

[326] *17th Annual National Survey of Police Chiefs & Sheriffs*, National Association of Chiefs of Police (2005).

[327] Gun Policy & Law Enforcement, PoliceOne, March 2013.

- "All the horror stories I thought would come to pass didn't happen ...I think it's worked out well, and that says good things about the citizens who have permits. I'm a convert."[328]
- "I ... [felt] that such legislation present[ed] a clear and present danger to law-abiding citizens by placing more handguns on our streets. Boy was I wrong. Our experience in Harris County, and indeed statewide, has proven my fears absolutely groundless."[329]
- "Virginia has not turned into Dodge City. We have not seen a problem."[330]
- "The concerns I had – with more guns on the street, folks may be more apt to square off against one another with weapons – we haven't experienced that."[331]

---

[328] Glenn White (President, Dallas Police Association), DALLAS MORNING NEWS, Dec. 23, 1997.

[329] John B. Holmes (Harris County Texas District Attorney), DALLAS MORNING NEWS, Dec. 23, 1997.

[330] Jerry Kilgore (Virginia Public Safety Secretary), FREDRICKSBURG FREELANCE STAR, Feb. 2, 1996.

[331] Dennis Nowicki (Chief of Charlotte-Mecklenburg North Carolina Police), NEWS AND OBSERVER, Nov. 24, 1997.

- "... to the best of my knowledge, we have not had an issue. I had expected there would be a lot more problems ... But it has actually worked out."[332]
- "Coming from California [where he was on the Los Angeles police force for 28 years], where it takes an act of Congress to get a concealed weapon permit, I got to Maine, where they give out lots of carrying concealed weapon permits, and I had a stack of CCW permits I was denying; that was my orientation. I changed my orientation real quick. Maine is one of the safest places in America. Clearly, suspects knew that good Americans were armed."[333]
- "It has impressed me how remarkably responsible the permit holders have been."[334]

---

[332] William Burgess (Lieutenant of the Calhoun County Sheriff Department), BATTLE CREEK ENQUIRER, Jan. 28, 2005.

[333] James Craig, *Detroit police chief: Legal gun owners can deter crime,* THE DETROIT NEWS, January 3, 2014.

[334] Colonel James Wilson (Director Texas Department of Public Safety), DALLAS MORNING NEWS, June 11, 1996.

CHAPTER 61

Most Americans support concealed carry.

Myth: Americans oppose concealed carry.

Truth:

- 56% of Americans say that more concealed weapons would make the country safer.[335]

---

[335] Gallup Poll, *Majority Say More Concealed Weapons Would Make U.S. Safer,* October 2015.

CHAPTER 62

There is a need for concealed carry.

Myth: People do not need concealable firearms.

Truth:

- A concealable handgun was used by the defender in 80% of gun defenses. And a quarter of the gun defenses occurred outside of the defender's hone.[336]
- 77% of all violent crime occurs in public places. This makes concealed carry necessary for more than three quarters of self-defense needs. Unfortunately, due to burdensome laws hindering concealed carry, people aren't able to defend themselves properly in public.[337]

---

336 Gary Kleck and Mark Getz. *Armed Resistance to Crime: The Prevalence and Nature of Self-Defense with a Gun*, 86(1) THE JOURNAL OF CRIMINAL LAW & CRIMINOLOGY, 1995.

337 *See* U.S. Bureau of Justice Statistics, *Criminal Victimization in the United States*, 1993; *see also* Gary Kleck and Mark Getz, *National Self-Defense Survey*, 1995.

PART XIV

GUNS AND CHILDREN

CHAPTER 63

More guns in the home does not mean that more kids are getting shot.

Myth: Children are dying because of their access to guns.

Truth:

- While the number of handguns per capita increased over 41% from 1981 to 2002, the number of fatal gun accidents for children ages 0 to 14 decreased by almost 83% during that same time period.[338]
- The often-cited statistic that 13 children are killed each day by guns includes "children" ages 19-24 and those who are adult gang members. If the definition of "child" is changed to those between birth and puberty, then only about 0.02 children per state per day were killed by guns.[339] In contrast, 1,446 children die per year in transportation acci-

---

[338] National Center for Health Statistics; Firearms Commerce in the United States, BAFTE, 20021/2002.

[339] *See* Center for Disease Control WISQARS Fatal injury Reports for 2013.

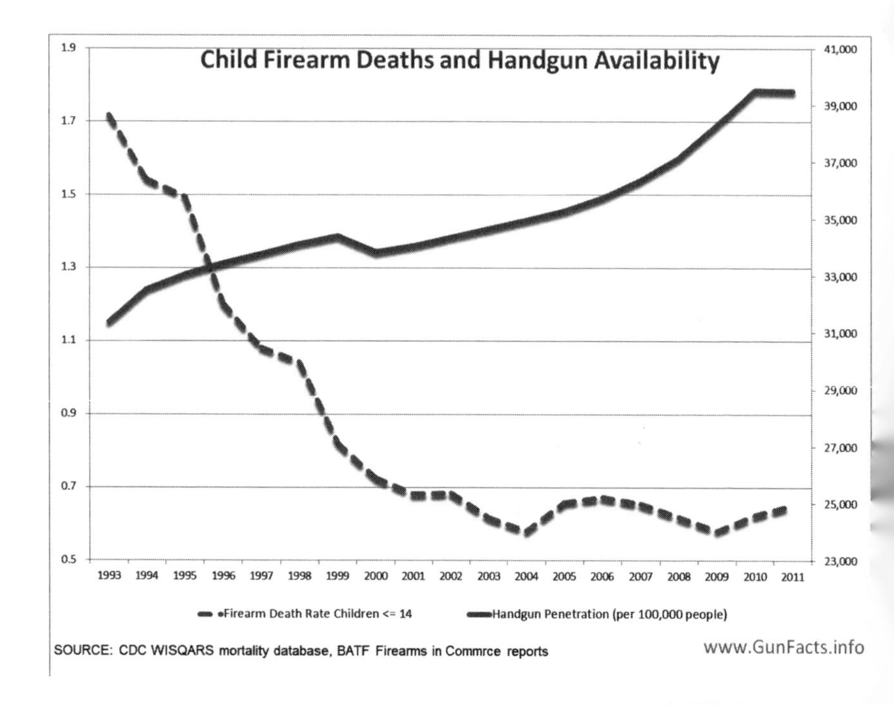

dents.[340] In sum, studies show that children under 14 are 12 times more likely to die in an automobile accident than from gun-related homicides.[341] And for the group ages 0 to 24, they are 8.6 times more likely to die in an automobile accident.[342]

---

340 *See* Center for Disease Control WISQARS Fatal injury Reports for 2012.

341 *National Vital Statistics Report,* National Center for Health Statistics, revised July 1999.

342 *Id.*

- Only slightly more than 1% of all unintentional deaths of children in the U.S. between ages 0-14 are from firearms.[343]

- The often-cited medical study purportedly showing that more kids are being shot as a result of more guns in the home has many flaws. It was published by a medical student who used a non-traditional database (not official records, such as those by the CDC). The medical student did not specify regional co-variance in gun ownership and, significantly, did not analyze other variables (multi-variant analysis). In sum, this study constitutes shoddy science.[344]

- Non-firearm related homicides of children exceed firearm-related homicides of children by almost a 5 to 1 ratio. And non-firearm juvenile violent crime in America is twice that of 25 other industrialized western nations. So we have a violence problem, not a "gun" problem when it comes to violent crimes committed against our youth.[345]

---

[343] *Deaths: Final Data for 2006,* National Vital Statistics Reports, Center for Disease Control, 2009.

[344] *See United States Childhood Gun Violence—Disturbing Trends,* Madenci, American Academy of Pediatrics.

[345] *See* FBI Uniform Crime Statistics, 1997; *see also Kids and Guns Bulletin,* Center for Disease Control and Prevention statistics, 2000.

- Boys who have legal possession to firearms tend to have much lower rates of delinquency and drug use than non-owners of guns.[346]
- The number of children protected by firearm owners far outweighs the number of children harmed by firearms each year. Firearms in civilian hands are used an estimated 6,849 times each day (or 2.5 million times a year) to prevent crime, including kidnapping, rapes, and aggravated assaults.[347]

[346] *Urban Delinquency and Substance Abuse,* U.S. Department of Justice, 2000.

[347] Gary Kleck, Criminologist, Florida State University, 1997.

CHAPTER 64

There is *not* an epidemic of school shootings.

Myth: School shootings are a huge threat to America's children.

Truth:

- James Alan Fox, the Lipman Family Professor of Criminology, Law, and Public Policy at Northeastern University, also found that schools today are safer than they were in the 1990s. Professor Fox's research led him to the conclusion that "There is not an epidemic of school shootings." Instead, as an article detailing Fox's findings explains, "[f]our times the number of children were killed in schools in the early 1990s than today." "[M]ore kids are killed each year from pool drownings or bicycle accidents. There are around 55 million school children in the United States, and on average over the past 25 years, about 10 students per year were killed by gunfire at school."[348]

---

[348] Allie Nicodemo & Lia Petronio, *Schools are safer than they were in the 90s, and school shootings are not more common than they used to be, researchers say*, NEWS@NORTHEASTERN, Feb. 26, 2018, HTTPS://NEWS.NORTHEASTERN.EDU/2018/02/26/SCHOOLS-ARE-STILL-ONE-OF-THE-SAFEST-PLACES-FOR-CHILDREN-RESEARCHER-SAYS/.

- "Compared to other types of violence and crime children face, both in and outside of school, school-based attacks are rare. While the Department of Education reports 60 million children attend the nation's 119,000 schools, available statistics indicate that few of these students will fall pretty to violent situations in school settings."[349]
- Over an eight-year period, there were 15 school shootings in states without "right to carry" laws. In contrast, there was only one school shootings in states that allow citizens to carry guns.[350]

[349] *Threat Assessment in Schools,* U.S. Secret Service and U.S. Department of Education, May 2002.

[350] Lott J, Landes W., *Multiple Victim Public Shootings, Bombings, and Right-to-Carry Concealed Handgun Laws: Contrasting Private and Public Law Enforcement,* University of Chicago – (covers years 1977 to 1995).

CHAPTER 65

Many problems plague the famous U.S. Department of Education study[351] finding that 240 schools had a school-related shooting in 2015-2016

Myth: According to a famous 2018 study done by the U.S. Department of Education, 240 schools had a school-related shooting in 2015-2016.

Truth:

- This "study" was so botched that the researchers logged 16 shootings of one school district when an NPR investigation showed zero. Moreover, in 161 cases, schools or districts testified that no incident took place. And in at least four cases, the incident did not meet the government's parameters for a shooting.[352]

---

[351] U.S. Department of Education, *School Climate and Safety,* April 2018.

[352] *The School Shootings That Weren't,* NPR, August 2018.

PART XV
STAND YOUR GROUND

CHAPTER 66

Stand Your Ground laws do not empower murderers.

Myth: 'Stand Your Ground" laws[353] turn people into bloodthirsty killers.

Truth:

- Attorneys Joseph Greenlee and Jonathan Goldstein studied the expansion of the castle doctrine in 2011, which strengthened its self-defense laws with a 'stand your ground' provision, and found:
  - "[T]here were 26,928 fewer violent crimes committed in the four years after the expansion's enactment than there were in the four years prior to its enactment. This resulted in a decrease in the violent crime rate from 391 per 100,000 population before the law to 329.8 after the law."[354]

---

[353] Stand-your-ground laws remove the duty to retreat in some cases of self-defense, and more than two-thirds of states have enacted some type of stand-your-ground law.

[354] Jonathan S. Goldstein & Joseph G.S. Greenlee, *Pennsylvania's Expanded Castle Doctrine: An Annotated Tour of the First Five Years,* 88 Pa. B.A. Q. 170, 178 (2017), available at https://docs.wixstatic.com/ugd/a979cf_2ba8ed4013bd40a8bd2a68e6501a9c35.pdf.

- "[T]here were 141 fewer murders in the first four years after the law's enactment than there were in the four years immediately preceding the law's enactment. The murder rate per 100,000 citizens also dropped significantly during that period, from 5.5 to 5.1. The decline in murders directly contradicts the argument that the expansion would encourage violence."[355]

- "[T]he percentage of persons charged with murder who were acquitted or had the charges dismissed remained virtually unchanged before and after the law's enactment—a direct refutation of the claim that the law provides 'gang-killers' and 'road rage killers' with 'get out of jail free' cards."[356]

- "[I]n the first full five years since the law's enactment (2012 – 2016), there were 10 justified homicides in which a criminal attacked a civilian. In the five full years immediately preceding the law's enactment (2006 – 2010), there were 12 . . . Clearly, the law did not convert emboldened

---

355 Jonathan S. Goldstein & Joseph G.S. Greenlee, *Pennsylvania's Expanded Castle Doctrine: An Annotated Tour of the First Five Years*, 88 Pa. B.A. Q. 170, 179 (2017), available at https://docs.wixstatic.com/ugd/a979cf_2ba8ed4013bd40a8bd2a68e6501a9c35.pdf.

356 Jonathan S. Goldstein & Joseph G.S. Greenlee, *Pennsylvania's Expanded Castle Doctrine: An Annotated Tour of the First Five Years*, 88 Pa. B.A. Q. 170, 179 (2017), available at https://docs.wixstatic.com/ugd/a979cf_2ba8ed4013bd40a8bd2a68e6501a9c35.pdf.

murderers into self-defense victims under the law. Nor did it turn victims who would ordinarily flee into bloodthirsty killers."[357]

- The "decrease of 27,793 in the number of burglaries, and 63.9 in the rate of burglaries, strongly suggests that the castle doctrine expansion effectively deterred burglaries."[358]

---

[357] Jonathan S. Goldstein & Joseph G.S. Greenlee, *Pennsylvania's Expanded Castle Doctrine: An Annotated Tour of the First Five Years*, 88 Pa. B.A. Q. 170, 179–180 (2017), available at https://docs.wixstatic.com/ugd/a979cf_2ba8ed4013bd40a8bd2a68e6501a9c35.pdf.

[358] Jonathan S. Goldstein & Joseph G.S. Greenlee, *Pennsylvania's Expanded Castle Doctrine: An Annotated Tour of the First Five Years*, 88 Pa. B.A. Q. 170, 180 (2017), available at https://docs.wixstatic.com/ugd/a979cf_2ba8ed4013bd40a8bd2a68e6501a9c35.pdf.